Colour & Texture in Needlelace

Frontispiece: Evening Light. Designed and worked by
the author in silk and wool. 12cm × 12cm

ROS HILLS

Colour & Texture in Needlelace

DRYAD PRESS LTD LONDON

Dedication
To my mother with thanks

Acknowledgment
Special thanks are due to the following people:
Denise, whose fault it all is!; all family and
friends for their help and support, typing and
correcting; my colleagues in the 'Lace World'; all
those students who kindly lent their work for
publication; and Pam Watts for constant encouragement and enthusiasm especially on the
black days!

A photograph of the 'Angel' piece first appeared
in the *Embroidery Magazine*, Summer, 1985.

Photographs by Franta Provaznik, Oxford.

ISBN 0 8521 9644 X

Typeset by Keyspools Ltd, Golborne, Lancs.
and printed in Great Britain by
Anchor Brendon Ltd
Tiptree, Essex
for the publishers
Dryad Press Ltd
8 Cavendish Square
London W1M 0AJ

Contents

Foreword

To be asked to write the Foreword to a lace book written by a friend and colleague seemed, at first, rather daunting. I watch bobbin lace-makers with admiration and, as Ros says in her Introduction, a certain awe, but my true feelings are of apprehension of ever trying to master all those bobbins. I sat down to read the book and, page by page, a story unfolds of marvellously creative lace made with only a needle and thread. The various sections cover the early history, the techniques, the equipment needed, colour, design and the seemingly endless possibilities, but most of all I felt that I could do it and wanted to start a piece of work there and then. This is surely the strength of this book. It is written with authority but Ros is able to convey all her joy and enthusiasm for the craft she loves.

The section on design is particularly helpful and takes the beginner through the step-by-step stages sometimes overlooked in design chapters. The more experienced workers are encouraged to take part in the thought process and supply ideas of their own. Here is a book to stimulate visual awareness and to show that creativity is not the prerogative of the chosen few. This is the basis of Ros's teaching and the excellent photographs of her students' work prove this.

All craft-workers are accused of hoarding vast quantities of fabric and threads—and books too—but I am sure this will be a treasured addition to any bookshelf.

Pam Watts

Introduction

When I was a child I loved painting by numbers. The picture came in a box with all the required paints and a paint brush. The little pots of oil paint had lids on them that were impossible to open. I often resorted to squeezing them in between a door and its frame with the usual awful result of the pot splitting and paint spattering down the wall and onto the carpet. My mother's remarks on discovering the mess shall not be reported here.

Art classes became my salvation at school, a haven away from dreaded maths and Latin; I have now gone on to enjoy using threads instead of paints as a way of expressing my love of colour. I am still painting by numbers the difference now being that the areas I fill with colour are stitched and not painted.

The world of lace-making opened up to me whilst I was taking a City and Guilds Creative Textile course. The particular aspect of lace that I fell in love with was Needlepoint. The technique of needlepoint lace, that is a fabric built up of buttonhole stitches in either simple or complicated combinations with some twisted threads, has in recent years played rather a secondary, even non-existent role to that of bobbin lace. Bobbin lace is made by plaiting, weaving and twisting threads which are kept in a set form by means of pins placed in prepared holes on a pattern. Bobbins are used to store the threads that are then run off the bobbins as needed.

Needlelace actually developed alongside bobbin lace in Europe, in the seventeenth century. Bobbin lace has always attracted public attention because initially it is so visually exciting.

Many bobbins are used together in one piece of work and are often decorated with painting and beading. English bobbins are attached at the end to a wire threaded with beads called a spangle, this weights the bobbin when in use. They can be made of ivory, ebony, glass or any wood or metal. The lace-maker who handles them is regarded in awe by anyone who has never seen lace being made before.

Needlelace however has none of this glamour. The lace-maker is possibly holding in her hand a small piece of fabric on the front of which she works a design that has been attached to a piece of PVC film or architects' linen. Only a needle and thread are being used to make the stitches and it is not immediately obvious that this is a lace in the making. However, if only the passer-by could be told that Venetian lace-makers put 6300 stitches into every square inch of their lace and that it often took years of hard labour to produce a length of needle-made lace, then their attitude to this lace might change.

Several countries claim to be the birthplace of the lace, notably Belgium and Italy. It is thought that the techniques perhaps came from Europe with the Crusaders returning from the Holy Land. The most wonderful laces were created using combinations of simple loop stitch to create many different patterns. These laces are considered to be far superior to the later bobbin laces.

Fig 1. Tree Stump. Worked by Val Palmer in wool, silk and cotton. Approximately 20cm × 10cm

It used to be that the amount of lace you owned denoted your social standing in society and consequently lace was a highly-prized commodity. Huge sums of money were paid for it, property being mortgaged and sometimes even sold to raise the necessary money for the purchase of the precious fabric.

Origins

Needlelace has its European origins in embroidery. During the thirteenth and fourteenth centuries in Europe geometric patterns were worked in coloured silks on a network of small square meshes. This was known as 'opus filatonium' and 'opus araneum' or threadwork and spiderwork. The work became known in Italy as 'square net point' and in France as 'lacis'. This form of embroidery led to the first needlelace being made called Reticella, although it is said that mummies excavated from Egyptian tombs had decoration on their clothing similar to Guipure lace and this is possibly the most ancient lacework in existence.

Reticella was followed by Punto in Aria, which means stitches in the air. A very evocative name. It was the first time that decorative patterns of thread, themselves forming a fabric, were created without being attached to a support fabric.

We have all seen pictures of the stiff ruffs that used to be worn around the necks of both men and women. On the edges of the ruffs was the stiffened geometric lace Punto in Aria. A good definition of lace is that it is a decorative material made of threads which are twisted, stitched and or plaited together without being attached to any fabric already woven.

The first laces were very flat and had charming designs of men and women with animals and plants. The designs look fresh and appealing even today.

The Roman church and the courts of Europe have always been the chief patrons of the lace-making industry. A ruff worn by King James 1 needed 25 yards of needlelace for its edging. In the time of Queen Elizabeth I lace was sometimes made of ladies' hair and called Point Tresse.

In the seventeenth century Venice was the main lace producing centre of Europe, the Venetian lace-makers making the heavy, richly decorated lace known as Venetian Gros Point. This lace contrasts with the very fine laces of the eighteenth century that were worn in great quantities by the nobility. However, the French Revolution saw the end of the extravagant wearing of lace. Where it had been highly prized it was now burnt in quantity for it was associated with the aristocracy and they were closely associated with the guillotine!

The decline of the lace-making industry was made complete by the invention of machines which made the fine nets used in the production of lace and then more machines which made the lace itself. This was a direct result of the Industrial Revolution which so affected many areas of the textile industry in Europe in the eighteenth century. In the very early twentieth century lace was still popular as a decorative addition to clothing, but from the 1920s onwards this popularity dwindled and fewer and fewer people were interested in making the lace or in using it.

Needlelace today

Until the last decade there was a danger that lace as an art form would be lost forever as there were hardly any lace schools or lace teachers who could pass on the knowledge. Today, however, all that has changed and we find that there are both day and evening classes in lace-making at nearly all Adult Education centres in the country. Traditions are being passed on and the new lace-makers are taking up the techniques and making lace that is exciting and totally different from its predecessors. There are now lace groups and guilds all over the British Isles with at least 7,000 known members. It is possible to attend lace weekend workshops, summer schools and lace days where the lace-maker's passion for beautiful bobbins and other hand-made tools of his/her trade may be purchased. Once again children are being taught at their mother's and grandmother's knees about the mysteries of lace patterns and stitches. Books are being written by

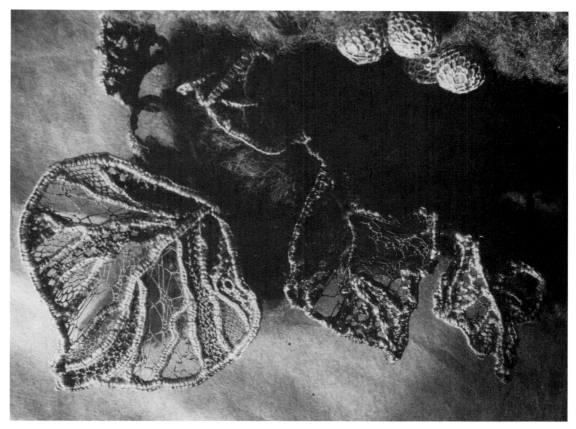

Fig 2. Close-up of Fig 1

today's lace-makers about not only the past glories of lace but also about the present and future glories. Nenia Lovesey has made the greatest contribution to the needlelace world with her books about the lace. For further study of the history of needlelace *The Technique of Needlepoint Lace* by Nenia Lovesey is essential reading. Nenia wrote the book with City and Guilds students in mind because at the time it was published there were no books available which encompassed the history, techniques and patterns which the student needed. The book, published by Batsford, has many beautiful photographs of old lace together with a great deal of historical information.

Unlike Nenia's book this one contains no photographs of old lace as it is intended to show some of the work being done by students and teachers in the field of creative needlelace. There are very few traditional stitches or techniques given as the idea behind the book is to inspire and encourage you to experiment yourself, taking the old techniques and extending them to reach new areas in creativity; making needlelace not just a craft but an art form too. In this way only can we keep the lace light burning, luckily not in the dark damp cellars of the past, where lace-makers suffered great hardship in the production of the work, but in the bright sunlit comfort of our homes and workrooms.

Work has already been started in this century with these thoughts in mind, we only have to look at the work of Virginia Churchill Bath, an American painter, needle-worker, designer, teacher and lecturer. Her book *Lace* should be on every aspiring lace-maker's bookshelf for the wonderful collection of photographs of modern lace that it contains. An inspiration to us all.

Fig 3. Flowers and butterflies

Fig 4. Stumpwork. Worked by Margaret Potts. *Memory of my grandmother*. Frame—random dyed silk fabric, plaited and then woven. Stitchery in silk

13

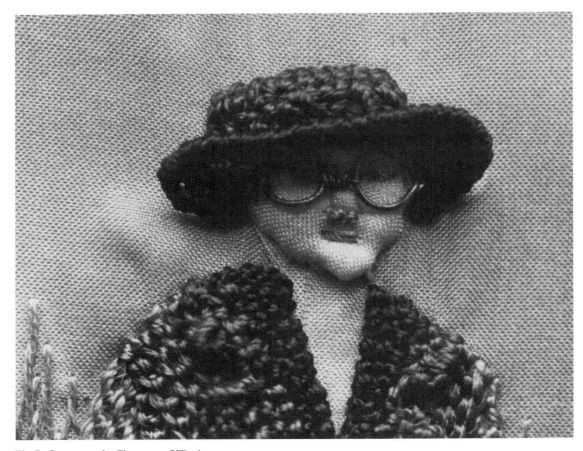

Fig 5. Stumpwork. Close-up of Fig 4

There are occasional exhibitions of lace where something exciting and different may be seen or there may be an article written about needlelace that has fresh and interesting ideas. There are also small groups of lace-makers striving to be creative, for example the Fritillary Group which is a branch of the North Downs Lace-makers, an active group in the South of England. The Fritillary Group meets four times a year. They set themselves a project for the following meeting, each member of the group having to design and make a piece of lace for that project. Each piece of lace is then shown to the group and its concept and method of construction is explained and discussed. This is a very positive contribution to the encouragement of creativity.

We are all capable of creativity but have this built-in feeling that we cannot design or transform our own ideas into a piece of work. We know what we like in terms of colours and shapes but have great difficulty in carrying out our ideas.

Many students have said to me that they just do not know where to begin when it comes to designing their own work. This book covers all the basic requirements involved in making lace, starting with equipment and stitches and then on to explain the mysteries of colour theory, use of coloured and textured threads and where to start when thinking about carrying out your own design. You may be just a beginner or you may be an experienced lace-maker with years of loyal service to your lace pillow behind you, whatever your current status I hope you will be stimulated by one aspect or another of this book.

Fig 6. Fritillary. Worked by the author in silk threads
and fabric. 7cm × 8cm

ONE

How Needlelace is Traditionally Made

How it is done

Needlepoint lace today may be made to any design and to any size. In America large-scale pieces of work are very much in evidence sometimes measuring up to eight feet square. Thick threads are used to create texture and interesting visual effects. In Europe the needlelace being made seems to be on a much smaller finer scale, however, it is just as free and exciting. This difference illustrates the tremendous adaptability of needlelace, a perfect medium for self-expression. Whether it is made in thick rope or fine silk, or even from strips of fabrics, it is still lace made using the traditional techniques.

The Alençon lace workshops of the eighteenth century housed approximately 13 workers, each person doing a different job in the production of a finished piece of lace. Today the lace-maker must carry out each stage in a logical sequence herself. The first step is to decide on a design to work and to draw it out on cartridge paper. Parchment is no longer easily obtained so a good quality cartridge paper must suffice for this purpose. A clear border of about two inches should be left around the design.

The design should be covered with some form of clear plastic sticky-backed film or architects' linen for ease of working with your needle and in order to protect the design. These materials should be available from good drawing office suppliers. See Suppliers list.

The design and the film or linen covering it are both tacked onto a piece of calico or waste fabric which has been folded into three thicknesses for

firmness. The lace design is now outlined with a double thread. This thread is called the cordonnet and is couched down onto the linen using a fine hand-sewing needle and a length of sewing cotton. The needle passes through the linen, paper and fabric and over the cordonnet. A fine needle will only make small holes in the linen that are less likely to tear through as you work the lace. If you need to use the same pattern more than once then it is advisable to use the architects' linen over your design as this will not wear as badly as the less durable plastic film.

The cordonnet must run in a continuous unbroken line around the whole of the design. There must be no breaks in the outline as this would show up as a weak point when the lace is removed from the backing cloth.

When the couching process is complete you will see that your design now has several different areas surrounded by thread. These areas are filled in with a series of buttonhole stitches called the fillings. By changing the number of stitches per loop and per row many variations of pattern may be achieved.

There are about 80 known traditional stitch patterns to choose from let alone any that you may design for yourself. Some of the basic stitches are shown in this book together with ideas about creating your own stitches.

When all the areas of your design have been filled in, the original cordonnet can be padded with several threads (crochet cotton is very suitable for this task) and close buttonhole stitched the whole way around the design. The close buttonhole stitching is called the cordon-

Fig 7. Section of waistcoat. Worked by Margaret Potts in dyed silk strips joined by Arabic stitch

Fig 8. Landscape in progress. Worked by the author in wool, cotton and silk. 20cm × 12cm

nette. The padding can be very thick creating a raised sculptured look as in the Venetian Gros Point, or the padding can just be one or two threads for an almost flat surround. Wire could be laid down with the core threads making sure that the wire you use is rust proof. This gives great flexibility to the lace especially if it is a larger piece and also, for example, where a butterfly's wings are required to stand out. They could be manipulated into graceful positions where the wire is present. The cordonnette covers the cordonnet completely. The process is explained in greater detail in a later chapter.

When the cordonnette is complete the lace is ready to be removed from its backing fabric. To do this simply pull apart the paper and film or linen from the fabric and, using a sharply pointed pair of embroidery scissors, cut through all the original couching stitches that passed through the fabric. The lace may now be lifted off the film.

You will notice that the small pieces of the couching thread are probably stuck in the back of the work. These pieces can be removed with a small pair of tweezers. Some of the pieces are quite hard to remove but gentle perseverence will succeed. The finished lace may now be put to its intended purpose which could be anything from appliqué on pillow slips to decorating a box lid as in this example by Pam Nether.

In Chapter 6 the whole process of starting and

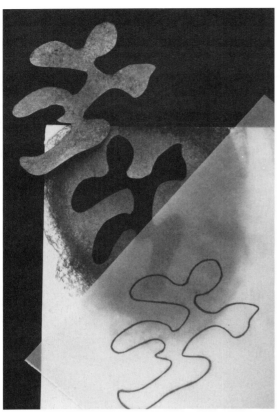

Fig 9. Dancing figures. Worked by Margaret Hamer.
1. Making a stencil

finishing a piece of lace is explained in greater detail.

Equipment

The equipment that you need to construct your lace is neither difficult to obtain nor expensive to make or buy. Unlike bobbin lace which often quickly involves the enthusiastic worker in collecting dozens of bobbins at an average cost of £2.00 each, all you need for needlelace is a needle and thread and some scraps of fabric.

Threads

Threads need to be chosen carefully as different threads are needed for different stages in the process of lace-making. In earlier centuries one of the threads used was a very fine linen. We in

Fig 10. Dancing figures. Worked by Margaret Hamer.
2. Print and thread winding

Fig 11. Dancing figures. Worked by Margaret Hamer. 3. Work in progress

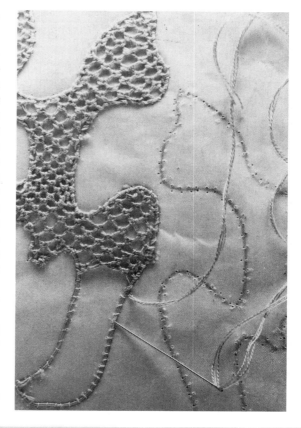

this century with all our technological achievements seem to have lost the techniques by which such a fine thread might be hand-spun in large quantities. The spinners of such a thread had to work in damp conditions with no proper light by which to work. Their working day often stretched over 12 hours to ensure a continuous fine quality of thread. It is no wonder that the workers, who were mainly women, were nearly blind by the time they were in their thirties. The coming of machine-spun yarn eliminated all this hard labour but the art of fine spinning was lost. The hand-spun thread was very expensive, one pound in weight of the best Antwerp linen cost £240.00 in the eighteenth century.

Today we have at our disposal easily obtainable threads of varying thicknesses and quality.

As a lace-maker you must first decide on the use of the finished piece of lace. It may be purely

Fig 12. Dancing figures. Worked by Margaret Hamer. 4. Two figures complete 8cm high

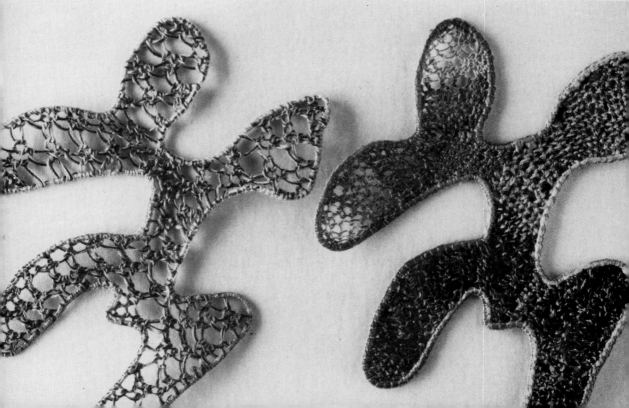

Fig 13. Box lid with needlelace. Worked by Pam Nether in silk and beads. 13cm × 9cm

Fig 14. Close-up of Fig 13

decorative and not be handled after it is complete or it may be part of a garment that will need to be laundered frequently. For hard wear a linen thread could be chosen but for decoration the options are very wide and you will probably choose threads in terms of colour and texture rather than strength.

Collecting threads
I think it is important to collect as wide a variety of threads as possible. If possible buy threads when and where you see them for use at a later

date. In this way you will quickly build up a collection varying in colour, texture and weight.

Storage can be a problem. Sometimes there are so many yarns that you forget what you do have in stock. Large empty plastic sweet containers, obtainable from your local newsagent or sweet shop, are very useful thread containers. They are light in weight and, of course, transparent so that, theoretically, you can see at a glance just what threads you have. Lined up on a shelf they can look very attractive.

You will quickly become aware of the fact that

20

Fig 15. Suitable threads for needlelace from top:
Silk thread size 200/3
Machine embroidery thread
Cotton thread size 30 Metler
Silk thread size 100/3
Metallic machine embroidery thread
Silk thread size 40
DMC cotton Perle size 12
DMC Cordonnet special size 15
Cotton perle
Courtelle
Soft cotton
Antique silk cord
Mohair with metallic thread
Rayon
Lurex
Silk ribbon
Knitting yarn with slub
Textured cotton knitting yarn

suppliers of interesting threads are few and far between. If you belong to a lace group or go to a regular class your group leaders or tutor should be able to supply you with a list of names and addresses of these suppliers. If, however, you do not have access to such a list then the one in this book may help you.

Traditional needlelace designs each have their own particular needs as far as threads are concerned, but when making a free-style modern piece of lace, there really are no rules. The one thing to say about threads is that when you are just beginning it is a good idea to use a firm single thread with quite a high degree of twist in it, for example the DMC cordonnet threads. The outline of your design needs a firm thread that will happily lie parallel with its neighbour during the couching process.

Needles

The needle that you use to make the greater part of the lace should not have a sharp point, this is to ensure that you do not split any of the threads when you are working them. I have discovered to my cost that split threads do make quite a difference to the look of the work if you are trying to create a smooth even effect. Therefore tapestry needles and hand-sewing ball-point needles are most suitable for filling in or working areas with buttonhole patterns. These may be purchased from any good haberdashery shop or department store. The size of the needle that you use will depend largely on the size of the thread that you are working with so it is best to keep a selection to choose from in your workbox.

For the couching process a fine sharp-pointed needle is required as it has to pass through all the layers of film, paper and fabric when couching down the cordonnet. Suitable needles are a crewel needle size 10, a between needle size 8 or a sharps needle size 8. The sharps needle is longer and finer than the betweens size 8.

Lace pillow

The next item on your requirement list is a lace pillow. It provides the lace worker with a firm base to work on and leaves both hands free to manipulate needle and thread. It seems to be easier to obtain an even working tension when both hands can be employed in this way.

It is possible to make your lace holding it in your hands throughout the process, the only way to find our how you like to work is for you to try both methods. Most people find that a combination of working on the pillow and in the hands works well.

You can buy pillows from lace suppliers but this is an expensive way to obtain what you want. There are two easy ways of making them for yourself. For the first method you will need a large tin. A catering-size baked bean tin is the perfect size. You could perhaps haunt your local school kitchen exit or try and get to know a chef who could supply you with this item! Having found your tin you should now proceed to pad it around with some kind of padding, for example strips of an old blanket, pieces of towelling or even bought wadding will do. Pad the tin to a depth of $\frac{3}{4}$in (2cm) at least. This will allow for pins to be inserted through the edges of your work and into the padding for a firm hold. When the padding is thick enough you then need to make a tubular cover for the whole tin, preferably in a dull plain fabric, say blue or green. Jazzy geometric shapes on a piece of fabric left over from last summer's sun-dress are definitely not conducive to hours of peaceful work at your lace pillow!

Having sewn a piece of dark fabric into a tube, make a casing at each end of the tube and insert cotton tape through one casing and elastic through the other. Put your cover onto the padded tin. The cover should fit closely so that the end of the cover with elastic in the casing corresponds with the open end of the tin. Draw up the cotton tape and tie it in a secure bow tucking the bow and the ends of the tape under the fabric at the closed end of the tin. Draw up the elastic leaving a small hole that can be stretched open by your hand at the open end of the tin. You now have a perfect place in which to carry around not only your current piece of work but also threads, scissors, pins and even sandwiches! People on trains are always fascinated by the number of different things that appear from the interior or my lace pillow.

Another way to make a pillow is to buy from your local D.I.Y. shop a roll of polystyrene normally used for lining damp walls. At the time of writing a roll will cost you about £1.00. Cut off a section of the roll, approximately 9in (23cm) long. This will leave you with two-thirds of a roll of polystyrene intact to sell to other aspiring needlelace-makers!

Next cut out two circles of thin card to the diameter of your 9in (23cm) long cylinder and stick them, using Sellotape, over the cut ends of the roll. This avoids trailing broken polystyrene behind you as you carry your pillow around! You do not need to pad your cylinder as pins will stick easily into the polystyrene, simply cover the cylinder with a tubular cover as for the tin.

Having made your pillow you will need a piece of doweling approximately 7in long and $\frac{1}{2}$in in diameter to use as a support under your lace as you work it on the pillow. Doweling may be obtained from hardware shops.

Other equipment

Other pieces of equipment that you will find useful are a fine pair of pointed embroidery

Fig 16. Lace pillow and equipment

scissors, a fine crochet hook, a very small pair of pliers and possibly some sort of finger guard. A thimble may be what you like to work with, alternatively a leather finger shield may easily be made from a few scraps of leather or suede. They are supple and easily replaced if, like me, you are prone to losing things.

More specialist equipment such as a couronne stick may be purchased from lace suppliers. A couronne is a buttonholed ring that was added to finished lace for extra decoration and texture. In order to make these rings of different sizes a graded stick has been produced, made of hardwood with shoulders cut into the wood, graduating in size from $\frac{1}{4}$ to $\frac{1}{2}$in in diameter. You can buy quite plain ones or, if you are lucky enough to

know someone with a metal worker's lathe, you may be able to persuade them to make a more elaborate one for you.

There are other pieces of equipment that were traditionally used in the production of needlelace such as an afficot made from bone, ivory or wood. This tool was used to polish the raised parts of the cordonnette. It is also nice to have a couronne box, a small wooden box that will hold all those couronnes which were the wrong size for the piece of work they were made for. They might fit another design at a later date. Antique fairs are a good source of supply for this type of box.

A good working light is essential. You may be lucky enough to be able to work in the morning light but if, however, you have other daytime

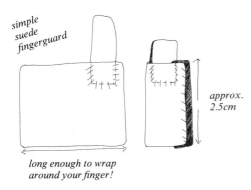

simple suede fingerguard

approx. 2.5cm

long enough to wrap around your finger!

Fig 17. How to make a simple finger guard

demands and have to make lace at night then make sure you have a firm chair that will support your back comfortably and an angle-poise light by which to work. It is possible to buy a light with a built-in magnifying glass but these are very expensive and not really necessary unless the work is very fine.

It is possible to buy small deep rectangular wicker baskets that have a lid and a carrying handle. These baskets are just big enough to take a needlelace pillow and all the accompanying equipment. You can line them and put pockets into the lining to take all the tools of your trade. A very satisfactory way of keeping everything together. Having assembled all your equipment you are now ready to make lace.

1
Angels. Worked in silk and gold kid by the author. 8cm × 6cm

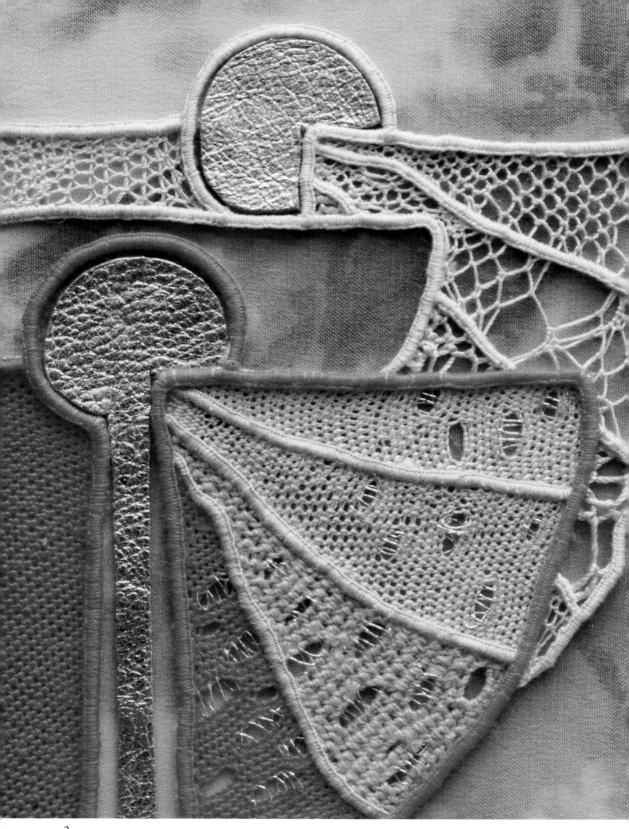

2
Landscape. In the process of being worked in wool and silk by the author

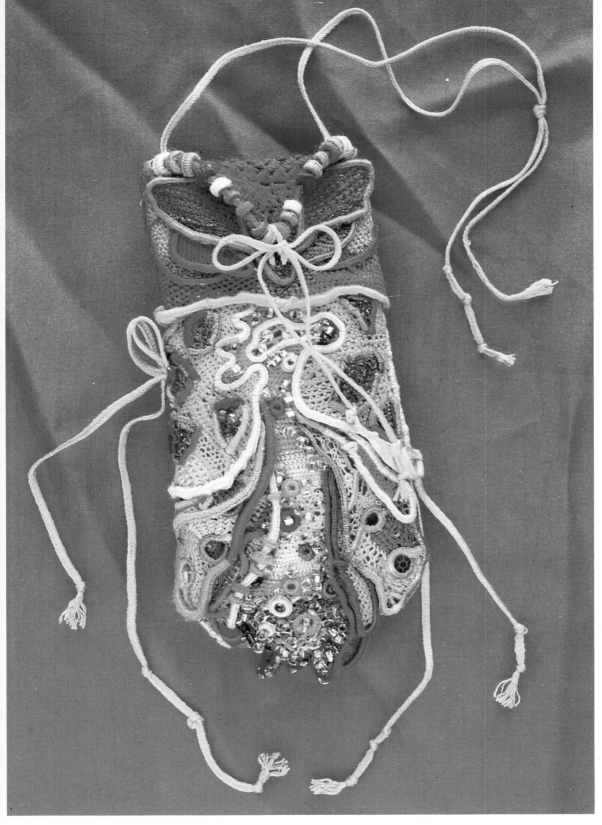

3
A purse worked in silks by the author. 6cm × 4cm. Purchased by the Victoria and Albert Museum, July, 1986

4
Branching bars worked in
wool, silk and metallic
threads by the author.
6cm × 4cm

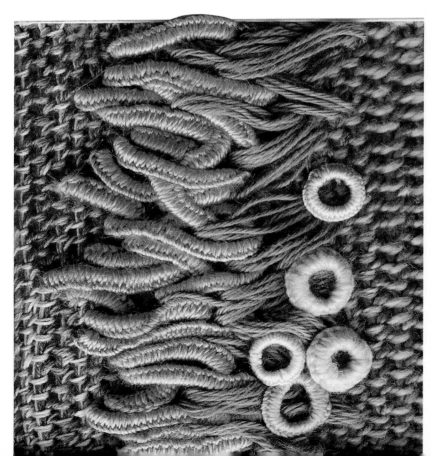

5
Buttonhole bars worked in
silk by the author.
6cm × 4cm

TWO

The Sampler

Samplers are often regarded by the workers as being the necessary evil that must come before the 'real thing' can be started. However, you only have to look at the beauty of the eighteenth- and nineteenth-century embroidered samplers to realise that, when carried out with imagination and care, a sampler can be a joy and a treasure in itself. They are especially valuable as records of work to their makers and could go on to fetch high prices in the auction rooms of the future.

It is with these positive thoughts in mind that you should prepare your sampler base. There are several ways of making a base to work on. One of the most attractive ways is to select a favourite colour in a narrow ribbon together with a piece of plain fabric in a similar or contrasting colour. The idea is that you will make up the sampler to have spaces for at least one dozen stitches. The spaces should be different sizes so that you can use different thicknesses of thread. It would seem obvious to use a large space for a thick thread

and a small space for a fine thread however, there is no reason why you should not reverse that and fill in the small spaces with a thick thread and the larger ones with a fine thread!

For a sampler having 12 one-and-a-half-inch square spaces on it you would need at least 4m of narrow ribbon. The choice of colours in ribbon is very good so it is an easy task to colour co-ordinate your ribbon and fabric. Choose a plain dark shade of fabric that has a smooth weave so that when you stitch your sample stitches their pattern will be clearly seen.

Making a sampler base

Cut and fold your fabric so that you have three layers of fabric with a finished outside edge

Fig 18. How to arrange ribbon on folded fabric base to use as a sampler

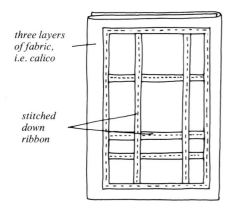
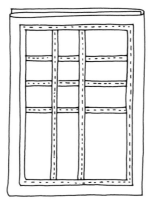
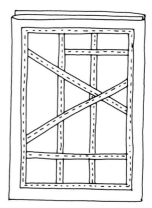

three layers of fabric, i.e. calico

stitched down ribbon

measurement of 6in × 8in (15cm × 20cm). Make sure that you hem the edges of the fabric before you start so that they do not fray. When you have your 6in × 8in (15cm × 20cm) shape you can then lay on your ribbon and decide how to arrange a pattern of spaces. See the following diagrams for a few suggestions.

Try drawing out your pattern and then transferring this to your fabric by drawing lightly with tailors' chalk and a ruler. These guidelines will show you exactly where to place your ribbon. Now sew the ribbon down, stitching through all the thicknesses of fabric using a sewing machine or backstitching by hand down the middle of each piece of ribbon. Make sure that you cover all the ends of the ribbon with the piece on the outside edge of the shape.

Having made your sampler base pin it securely to your pillow and slide your piece of doweling underneath it.

Beginning to stitch

Choose a coloured thread to match your ribbon and fabric. For example if you had a dark green fabric with a pale green ribbon then a pink thread would look attractive in stitching as pinks and reds are complementary in colour to greens. Choose a medium size thread, a DMC Cordonnet 60 would be a good size with which to start. You will also need a tapestry needle that will take the thread comfortably. I am often asked how much thread should be used to work with. A difficult question to answer. You should use whatever length of thread that you are comfortable with, taking into account the fact that a very long thread will tangle and knot as you use it and a very short one will use up very quickly. Remember also that you cannot easily join a new thread in the middle of a row of stitches. Approximately 18in (46cm) of thread is a good length to have in your needle.

I have included six traditional stitches for you to use as a starting point. There are many more but, as this book is concerned mainly with the way in which you can use these stitches, in a contemporary way, you will have to consult

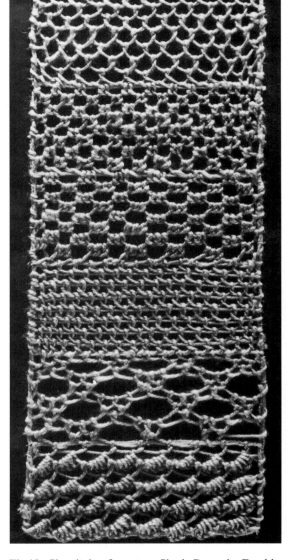

Fig 19. Six stitches from top: Single Brussels; Double Brussels; Treble Brussels; Corded stitch; Pea stitch; Cinq Point de Venise

other books to find the others. I would recommend all of Nenia Lovesey's books as well as *Lace* by Virginia Churchill Bath, and any old sewing manuals that you can find such as the Thérèse de Dillmont book. These may be found in second-hand book shops or may be ordered from specialist book suppliers.

First stitch

For your first stitch make the single Brussels stitch. This will get you used to using the needle and thread and to using both hands to control the tension of the stitches. When starting any stitch simply pass your needle underneath and up through the ribbon at the side of the shape you are about to fill in. Repeat this so that the thread is 'whipped' up the side of the ribbon ready to begin. You can now make a row of stitches along the edge of ribbon, going across the top of your shape. When you reach the other side of the shape whip the thread through the ribbon on this side and then return making stitches across the row to your starting point. Repeat until the space is full. Almost all the stitches shown in this chapter should be started in this way.

When working the stitches use a variety of threads including fine cotton, thick cotton, metallic threads, woollen threads of all textures and silk threads. It is only after experimenting with threads in this way that you will discover exactly in which thread you like to work.

Single Brussels stitch

1st row Whip around the ribbon on the left-hand side of a chosen space on your sampler. Make single buttonhole stitches along the top edge of the shape. Try to keep the stitches evenly spaced apart. Go under and through the ribbon on the right-hand side of the shape.
2nd row Make single buttonhole stitches into the loops made in the previous row. Work from right to left. Continue with rows 1 and 2 until the whole space is filled.

Having filled one space now go on to fill another, this time using a double Brussels stitch with a thicker thread. To make this stitch work two buttonhole stitches closely together, leave a space of two stitches, make another pair of buttonhole stitches and continue like this across your row. On the second row make your pairs of buttonhole stitches into the loops of the previous row.

Treble Brussels stitch simply has groups of three buttonhole stitches where there were two in the double Brussels stitch.

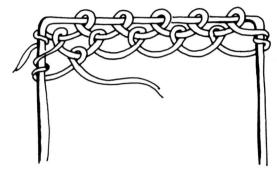

Fig 20. Single Brussels stitch

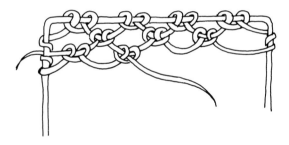

Fig 21. Double Brussels stitch

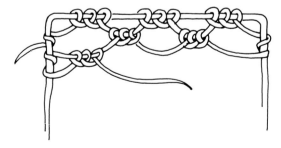

Fig 22. Treble Brussels stitch

Corded stitch

This stitch is a very versatile and simple one. All the early Venetian lace-makers used it for the closely stitched fillings of the designs. By spacing your stitches out or making them close together you can alter the appearance of the stitch quite dramatically.

1st row 1. Make a row of single Brussels stitches across the top of the area to be filled working from left to right.

2. Take your working thread under and over the cordonnet or ribbon twice.

2nd row Take the working thread back to the side that you started from.

3rd row Make buttonhole stitches into the loops of the 1st row picking up the laid thread of the 2nd row as you work.

Repeat the 2nd and 3rd rows for the pattern.

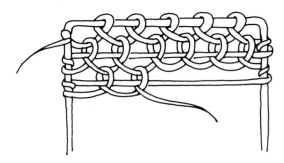

Fig 23. Corded stitch

Pea stitch

The delightfully named Pea stitch has many attractive variations. The stitch given here is one of the most well known.

1st row 1. Make a row of evenly spaced buttonhole stitches from left to right.

2. Take your working thread under and over the cordonnet or ribbon.

2nd row 1. Working from right to left make a stitch into each of the first two loops of the 1st row.

2. Miss the next to loops.

3. Make a stitch into the next two loops.

Continue like this across the row and then pass your working thread under and over the cordonnet.

3rd row 1. Make one stitch into the loop between the pairs of stitches in the 2nd row.

2. Make three stitches into the long loops in the 2nd row.

3. At the end of the row go under and through the cordonnet or ribbon.

4th row Make a stitch into each of the two loops formed by the groups of three stitches in the 3rd row.

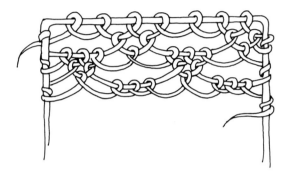

Fig 24. Pea stitch

Repeat the 2nd and 3rd rows to make the pattern.

Belle Point de Venise—cinq point

This is a more textural stitch and can be used to great effect when making a landscape design. For example if large quantities of threads are used together in a large tapestry needle, say six shaded threads, the stitch can be used to represent distant shrubs, bushes or hedges.

1st row Working from right to left make a row of buttonhole stitches leaving three stitch spaces between each stitch.

2nd row 1. Make a buttonhole stitch into the first loop of the first row.

2. Make five buttonhole stitches into the loop just formed, that is, to the left of the stitch you

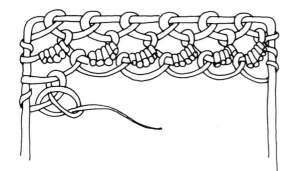

Fig 25. Cinq Point de Venise

have just made.

3rd row Make a row of buttonhole stitches, one stitch between each group of five stitches.

Repeat the 2nd and 3rd rows to form your pattern. Traditionally each group of five stitches should be the same size.

The six sitches just described form the basis of nearly all the work shown in this book.

Picots and couronnes

When you have filled in all the areas on a piece of work the final, and I think most exciting, part of the lace-making process is carried out. This process is putting on the cordonnette. As has already been explained this gives the final outline to your design. The cordonnette may simply be buttonhole stitches packed closely together, however it may also be heavily decorated with picots and couronnes.

Picots

Picots are projections along the knot side of the cordonnette. They can consist of just one elongated stitch or of a series of buttonholed loops or even of buttonholed bars. In order to experiment with picots and loops on a cordon-nette on your sampler, you should lay down about ten threads of, say, size 30 cordonnet across one of the squares on your sampler. You should actually whip a thread around the laid

threads and through the fabric of the sampler so that the threads may be held together in a roll. Three picots are given here for you to try: the simple picot; a loop picot; and a Venetian picot.

Simple picot

1. Make ten close buttonhole stitches along your laid threads.
2. Take a pin and put it into the base fabric underneath the threads of the cordonnette, and into your lace pillow.
3. Take your working thread under and around the pin and then over and under the threads of the cordonnette to the left of the pin.
4. Take your working thread above the cordon-nette and to the right.
5. Make a buttonhole stitch to hold the picot by putting your needle under the loop around the pin, over the pin and under the thread that comes from underneath the cordonnette.
6. Finally go over the thread that formed the loop to the right above the cordonnette.
7. Pull your thread tight to form the picot.
8. Make another buttonhole stitch to keep the picot in position.

You can create different effects by putting in different numbers of stitches between each picot or by having your pin at different distances from the edge of the cordonnette.

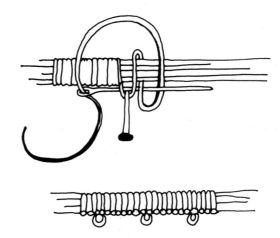

Fig 26. Simple picot

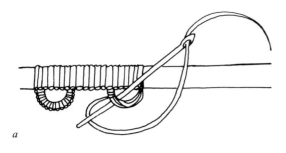

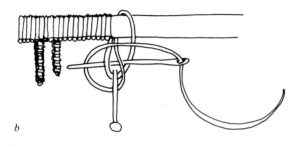

a

b

Fig 27a and **b.** Loop picot and Venetian picot

Fig 28. Picots

Loop picot

A loop picot is made by working your buttonhole stitches to where you want to start your loop and then following the instructions given below.

1. Take your needle back, for example, six stitches and pass it through the seventh stitch knot on your cordonnette.

2. Bring the thread back to the last buttonhole stitch made and pass your needle through its knot.

3. Return the thread to the seventh stitch and pass it through the knot again.

4. Buttonhole stitch along the loop of three threads you have just made and continue with the original cordonnette for eight stitches. Repeat stages one to four for more loops. The size of the loops depends on the number of stitches under each one.

Venetian picot

The Venetian picot can be made in the same way as the first simple picot except that the pin is placed further away from the cordonnette. The first buttonhole stitch is made close up to the pin and then more stitches are made down the loops until the cordonnette is reached.

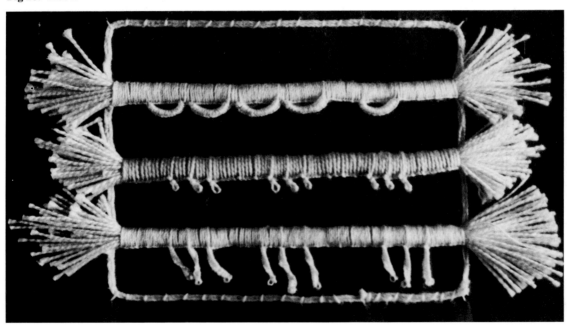

Interesting effects can be created by varying the lengths of the picots and by adding beads to them as you work.

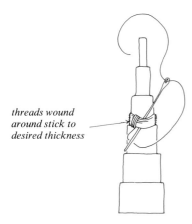

threads wound around stick to desired thickness

Fig 29. Couronne worked on a stick

Fig 30. Needlelace panel. Worked by Celia Batjoris in silk threads. Approximately 16cm²

Couronnes

These are buttonholed rings of thread that may be made either on a special couronne stick made for the purpose or on a pencil or chopstick or, for very tiny couronnes, a darning needle.

The couronne stick is made of hardwood and is graduated in size from being only ¼in (7mm) diameter at one end to being ½in (13mm) diameter at the other. At ½in (13mm) intervals along its length there are shoulders' cut into the wood especially for the thread to rest on.

To make a couronne
1. Take a length of thread 18in (45cm) long.
2. Wind the end of the thread around the chosen size of 'shoulder' on the stick. The number of times that the thread is wound around the stick will determine the final thickness of the couronne.
3. Make three buttonhole stitches into and around these threads.
4. Gently ease the threads up the stick to the next smallest 'shoulder'.

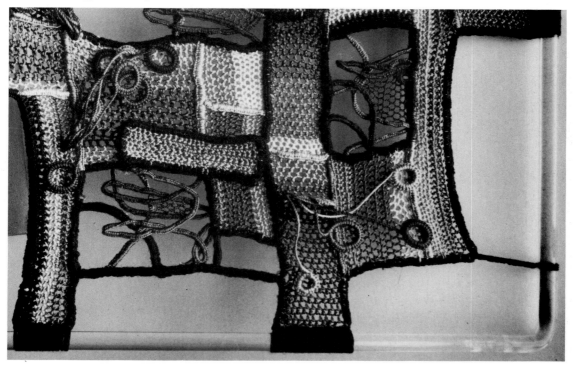

5. Continue buttonholing around the threads until the couronne is complete.

6. Take the couronne off the stick and pass the needle and thread down through the first knot of the first buttonhole stitch made and along the back of the stitches.

7. Leave a length of working thread for attaching the couronne to your finished lace.

Sizing

To make your couronne the correct size for the pattern you are working, simply lay your stick over the drawn circle on the pattern and move the stick until the edges of the circle can just be seen clearly either side of the stick.

Couronnes may be decorated with beads or they may have loops and or picots around them.

It is a useful exercise not only to practise making rows of stitches across squares and rectangles, but also to practise making stitches fill areas that are round, oval or of uneven shape. To do this you should draw several shapes, that is, a circle, an oval and a triangle and cover these with PVC film or architects' linen. Tack the paper and film to a fabric base and outline the shapes with a cordonnet. You can now fill in the shapes with stitchery increasing and decreasing the number of stitches per row as you work down the shape.

Fig 31. Close-up of Fig 41

THREE

Colour Theories

When thinking about working in colour do you experience a kind of sinking feeling or even a feeling of panic at the thought of trying to select colours for a piece of work? These feelings can easily be overcome. All you need to know are a few basic colour rules to feel that you could, in fact, create a colourful piece of work that looks 'right'.

As you begin to think about colour it is perhaps interesting to realise that colour actually affects our moods and emotions and our physical selves as well. Try to imagine that you have gone to your doctor feeling very unwell and that, when you walk into the surgery you find that the whole room has been painted a bright red. The furniture is emerald green and the carpet a zig-zag pattern of red and green. How would this onslaught of colour make you feel? How does it make you feel just thinking about it?

Most people decide on a fairly neutral colour scheme with which to surround themselves. We prefer to dress in neutral tones and earthy shades using the odd splash of bright colour occasionally. Our houses are more often than not also fairly neutral in overall interior colour, people fearing perhaps that they will become bored too quickly by having bright colours around them. This seems to imply that nature itself is colour shy but in fact nothing could be further from the truth.

If you think about a bank of azaleas flowering in the spring or even a barrow-load of fruit in a vegetable market you quickly realise that nature is both exciting and stimulating in her use of colour. The amazing colours of birds and but-terflies and sunsets are all there for us to see and to use in our work. There is sometimes a feeling that perhaps the quieter, more subtle colours are more serious and can therefore give a piece of work more authority and sophistication; an idea left over perhaps from the days when only the rich could afford to wear cream and white clothes because only they could afford to have their clothes professionally cleaned and laundered. Bright unlikely colour mixes in lace-making are sometimes considered not to be serious. Is there such a thing as the lace snob?

In the Far East colour is used unremittingly, I am thinking in particular of the use of brilliant colours by the people of Thailand and India and their use of flowers to complement clothing and important occasions. We need to get away from the idea that a colour scheme can be wrong, that you cannot put certain colours together. We should go forward with confidence and take as our guide nature herself, a past mistress at putting the 'wrong' colours together to great effect. The blue spines of delphinium in a summer border should lay to rest forever that old addage 'blue and green should not be seen'.

How, therefore, should we begin to sort out what colours we like best and what colours are produced when they are mixed with other colours. The theory of colour is usually demon-strated using a circle as a starting point. It would be a good idea at this stage to take a compass and A4 sketch book and collect together a selection of coloured felt-tip pens. When these materials are assembled you are ready to draw out your colour wheel. It is possible to buy colour wheels

Fig 32. Seahorse. Worked by Jane Meade. Frog. Worked by Denise Emmerson. Butterfly. Worked by Denise Emmerson in silks and cottons. 6cm

Fig 33. Landscape. Worked by Denise Emmerson. 15cm × 10cm

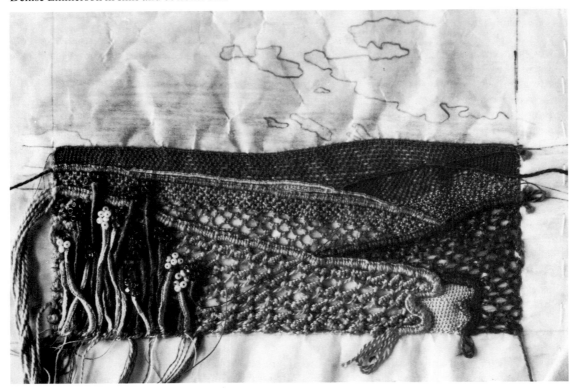

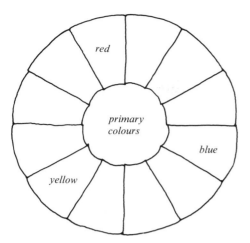 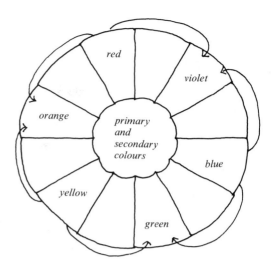

Fig 34. Colour circle with primary and secondary colours

from art shops but there is nothing like actually doing something yourself for making you remember the relevant facts.

Primary colours

To begin with draw a circle, using the compass, approximately three inches in diameter. Now divide the circle into 12 equal parts. Begin to colour in the parts on the circle, starting anywhere, with the primary colours. These are red, blue and yellow. Leave three spaces between each colour.

It is worth pointing out a few interesting facts about colour and about the symbolism of colour.

Red is the strongest hue in the spectrum. It is a positive colour and can create excitement and aggressivenes in people. Hardly the way sick people in a doctor's waiting-room wish to feel!

The colour blue is a cool, passive and tranquil colour and purports to stand for hope and serenity.

Yellow is the least popular colour of the spectrum. It has a split personality and so, while it is a cheerful pleasant colour much used by the impressionist painters, it is also used to denote cowardice and deceit. Traditionally Judas Iscariot wore yellow clothing.

Secondary colours

When these primary colours are mixed together in equal proportions they make what are known as secondary colours. Red and blue together make violet, blue and yellow make green and yellow and red make orange. Fill in these secondary colours in the middle section of the three empty sections between each pair of primary colours.

Violet has always been considered a rich stately colour. It can be made from a particular type of sea snail that used to be very expensive to buy. In fact the snails were said to be worth their weight in gold and consequently only the very rich could afford the dye made from these creatures. It can be both a cool and a warm colour and is used in religious clothing especially associated with Easter.

Green is a neutral colour and does not provoke particular emotions. It denotes freshness and youthfulness and peace. It is a restful colour to live with. The doctor's waiting room should have been painted pale green for extra calm patients!

Orange, made from red and yellow is not a very popular colour and has no real symbolic meaning. It is a warm colour and can be vibrant when used with its opposite in the colour wheel, blue.

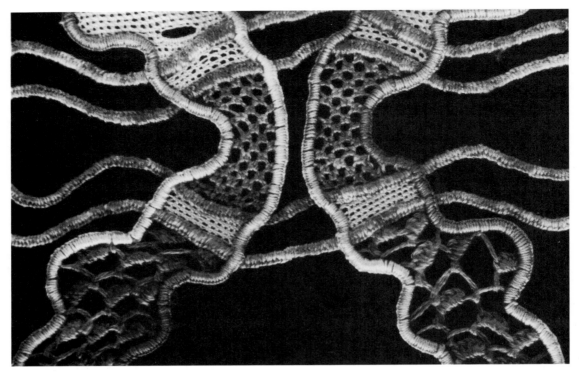

Fig 35. Abstract. Worked by Denise Emmerson in space-dyed cotton. 19cm × 7cm

Sub-secondary and tertiary colours

Having filled in the secondary colours you will be left with six empty spaces on your colour wheel. In these spaces go the sub-secondary colours, that is the colour obtained when the two colours either side of each empty space are mixed together.

If the secondary colours are mixed together you get what are known as the tertiary colours. These are olive, citron and russet.

If you want to *lighten* a colour to obtain a *tint* you must mix that colour with white, to *darken* it to get *a shade* you mix black with the colour. To make the colour more *neutral* then mix grey with it. This would be a *tone*. People tend to surround themselves with tints, tones and shades of colour rather than pure colour.

Colours have personalities, for example a warm colour scheme would be one where

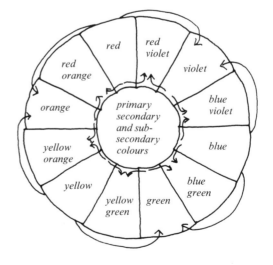

Fig 36. Colour wheel showing sub-secondary colours

36

Fig 37. Reverse colouring of an abstract design

browns, reds and yellows are used, whereas a cool colour scheme would be composed of blues, whites and greens. It is also worth noting that warm colours seem to come towards us whereas the cool colours recede into the background. If, therefore, you stitched an area in a dark blue colour it would look smaller in size than if it were stitched in a light yellow.

The following design has been coloured in in two different ways, the dark and light areas have been reversed to show how the design can apparently change just by the different use of dark and light colour.

Using threads instead of paints to mix colours

This is the briefest introduction to colour theory but there should be enough information to start you off experimenting with threads instead of coloured felt-tip pens. Choose an empty square on your sampler and take a coloured thread. Begin to work across your square in corded stitch to a distance of one third of the way down the square. Now take a length of white thread, sewing cotton will do, and thread it together with

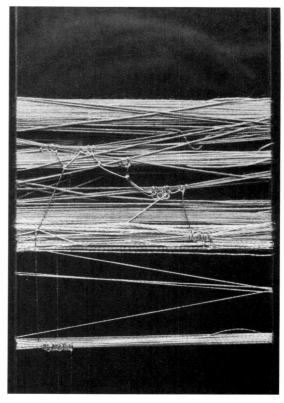

Fig 38. Perspex wrapped with threads and stitched. Area of wrapping 2cm × 3cm

the colour already in your needle. Continue sewing for another third of the square. At this point substitute a black thread for the white thread and use it with the original colour to finish the square. You will be amazed at how, when you hold your sample at a distance, the original colour has changed where the black and white threads were added.

You could now try mixing primary colours to get secondaries. Using the corded stitch and two needles, one thread in one colour which should be used for the return laid thread and the other coloured thread used for the buttonhole stitches.

It will soon be seen from making these simple stitch excercises that you do not in fact need to purchase very many different colours of threads. We should use fewer threads and mix them much more. After all in nature there is virtually nothing that is one flat colour, on close observation even the reddest of poppy petals can be seen to have a whole range of reds on its surface.

FOUR

Observing Your Surroundings

Trying to reproduce in lace what you see around you in the natural or even unnatural world can be a difficult and somewhat daunting task. Most people would agree that it is not simply a matter of looking at an object, for example a flower, and saying 'well this buttercup is yellow and it has green leaves with a green stem' and then choosing a yellow thread and a green thread and working a buttercup. The finished lace will look stiff and very 'dead'. It will not really look anything like a buttercup. A much closer observation of the original would have shown you that there are many shades of yellow in the petals, ranging from dark to light. The leaves are also many shades of green with pale green veins.

Colour winding

To help you to sort out these colours I would suggest that you make a colour winding with threads of the nearest possible colour to the flower. The threads may be textured or flat but should be colour-matched to the flower as closely as possible. Having raided your thread box for threads that you think match the flower, you should then cut a piece of card 1in wide and 4in long. On one side of this piece of card you should stick a piece of double-sided Sellotape and then:
1. Place your flower in front of you and although it is a three-dimensional object try to see it as a flat two-dimensional one.

Starting at the top of the flower pick out a thread that matches the colour at the rim of the petal. Call this your first area of colour.

lines show proportions of colours in flower head

Fig 39. Flower head showing proportions of colour

2. Peel back the backing from the double-sided Sellotape and stick one end of your chosen thread to the Sellotape at the top of the piece of card.
3. Begin to wind the thread around the card so that each line of thread lies immediately next to the previous one.
4. When you have wound your first colour for a distance in proportion to the amount of colour in area one, simply stick the end of the thread that you are using down onto the Sellotape at the back of the card and leave it to be picked up later when you want to use the same colour.
5. Match your next piece of thread as near as possible to the second area on your flower and begin to wind the thread around the card, sticking down the starting end of the thread.

As you wind the new thread around, it covers the end of the first thread that you used and carries it forward rather as you would carry colours forward in knitting. Continue down your

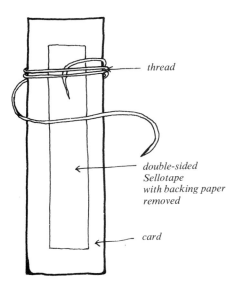

Fig 40. Starting a colour winding

Fig 41. Landscape. Worked by Pam Nether in silks, cottons and metallic threads. 20cm × 10cm

card choosing appropriate colours as you go to match different levels of colour in your flower. If you do not have an exactly matching thread try splitting your threads and mixing the strands together to get the mid tones that you need.

When you have colour-matched all the areas of the flower, end the winding by sticking down your last piece of thread and cutting it off together with any others carried forward.

Lay the winding next to the flower and look at the two together firstly from a distance and then really closely to see if you have left any colours out. The winding shows you how your threads will look together and how they balance each other.

Try to make a colour winding before starting a new piece of work in the same way that you might hunt through pattern books for a dress pattern and then search for fabrics and threads with which to make up the garment, or as you might make a tension square before knitting, a very important though often overlooked task. Preparatory work is always very worthwhile and increases your ability to observe your environment closely, a useful habit to cultivate that helps

in the development of your own design work. Be prepared however to become a real nuisance to your friends and family as you grovel around on your hands and knees when out on walks shrieking about the 'hundreds of colours on this fungi dear!' You will find that your companions will become accustomed to these activities in time!

Landscapes—where to find them!

When you have successfully completed your first lace flower you may be tempted to stretch your needlelace skills and try depicting a favourite

40

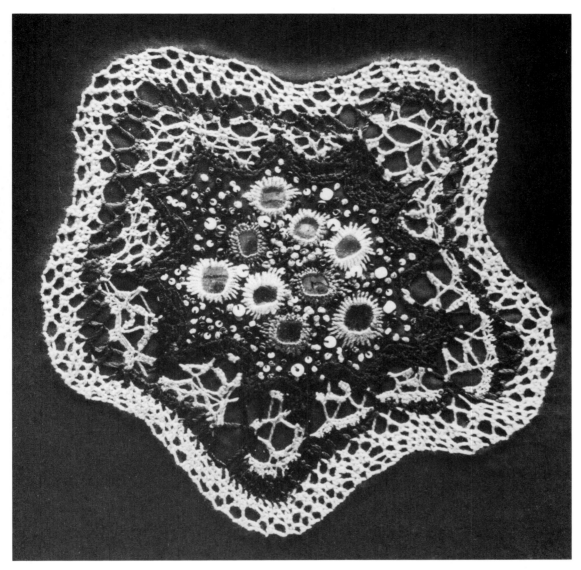

landscape. If you cannot easily observe the real thing start by looking at photographs and magazine pictures. Look in museums and art galleries even libraries and observe how other people have drawn, stitched or woven landscapes. Look at traditional scenes with trees and flowers and water running by and then look at the not so traditional where the artist has made the sky pink and the trees a strange shape.

Two marvellous examples of idyllic embroidered landscapes may be seen in the Victoria

Fig 42. Slice of life. Worked by Gill Martin. Detached stitcher and shisha glass

& Albert Museum in the corridor nearest to the textile study room. They are in a glass showcase there. They are approximately ten inches square and depict seventeenth-century life. They show a castle and a man and woman wandering in a sun-filled garden. The joyous things in life are shown to be the same size as the figures, for example the flowers are very large, totally out of proportion to the size of the castle. Life is shown as being all pleasure and sunshine. A reflection perhaps of the embroiderer's thoughts and feelings at the time.

When thinking about a landscape try to make some decisions as to whether you want to try to depict the whole of a scene or a small part of it. What will the season be? A bleak winter scene or a bright summer one?

Choice of colour

Colours should ring true, in other words be careful to avoid the 'chocolate box' syndrome, where the colours are bright and harsh and the sky shown a vivid blue. The skies over the British Isles are more often than not a pale grey rather than bright blue and the sun is not always shining, although having said that your mood can greatly affect your personal view of your surroundings.

Colours of trees and rocks and grass are usually tones of colour rather than bright hues.

Try not always to think of the obvious and easiest thing to do. A landscape could be one of your imagination where the sky is green and the grass is blue and where the roles of animals and birds are reversed, a little unusual but mind stretching.

Focal points

Your landscape should have a focal point. The horizon line itself if you are showing one is a good focal point, not necessarily, however, in the centre of the picture. Try not to make a design that can be divided equally in half either horizontally or vertically. This will make a dull composition. To avoid this try to position horizontal lines and shapes nearer to the top or bottom of the scene and put in vertical and diagonal lines at some distance from the centre of the picture as shown in diagram.

Notice too when you are next in the great outdoors that the sky is often very light at the

Fig 43a. Dull composition

Fig 43b. Interesting composition

Fig 44. Landscape enlarged foreground

horizon and the land very dark. You will see this phenomenon best when looking across large areas of flat land or indeed when looking out to sea. A hilly landscape though has its distant hills paler than those in the foreground.

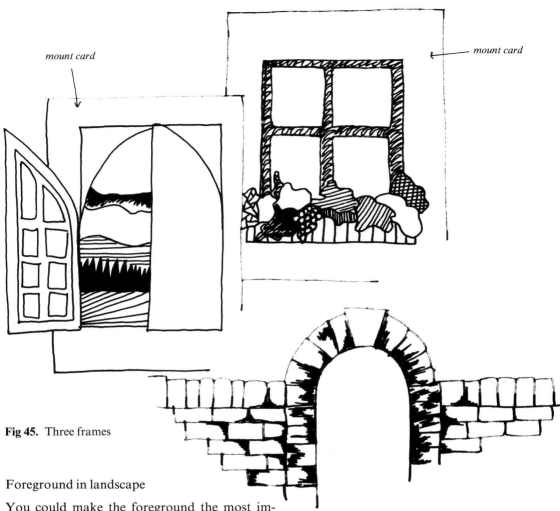

mount card

mount card

Fig 45. Three frames

Foreground in landscape

You could make the foreground the most important feature of your work as if you were lying down in the ground and had just parted the grass with your fingers. How big the daisies seem at such close range, the view of distant hills seen through these flowers is made all the more interesting.

It is always an effective ploy to include an element of mystery into a piece of work. A winding path, a darkened archway, a half-opened door or window. A path that disappears behind a building or shrub or tree leaving the viewer wondering where it leads. This kind of mysterious scene holds the viewers's attention far longer than one where all is revealed at once.

Framing

Having worked your design you then need to give thought as to how you might frame it. The frame could be worked as part of the lace or could be something quite separate. It could be an archway, a doorway or a window frame.

You might consider suspending your lace within a wooden surround or even sandwiching it between layers of glass or perspex. If you want to use a card mount you may wish to decorate the card in some way. You could paint the card, or sew threads onto it. Punch holes on the edges of the card and wrap threads through the holes and

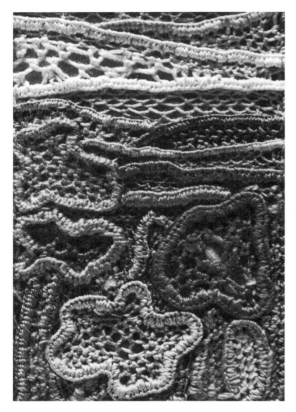

Fig 46. Landscape. Worked by the author in silks. 6cm × 4cm

Having given the subject of landscapes some thought and having carried out some exercises in observation, collect together all the photographs, postcards and magazine cuttings that you like and spread them out on the floor.

Look at your accumulated pictures and ask yourself why you like one view more than another. Is it the balance of colours one against another or perhaps the composition of hills against a sky? Is it the close-up views of mushrooms and leaves and flowers in a foreground or perhaps the wild colour schemes of a favourite painting by Van Gogh that appeal? Pick out at least six pictures that you like and then continue to narrow down your choice until you are left with one that pleases you in every way. This is the one to work.

This constant analysis is a habit that you can quickly develop. Another place for interesting patterns is your local zoo. Go along armed with a camera and a sketch book and pick out at least a dozen different patterns on as many animals and either photograph or sketch the design shapes. For example the amazing stripes on a zebra, the colourful markings on monkeys and the glorious pattens of a tiger's silky pelt. These are a fraction of the design sources available to you.

There are hundreds of books published about the natural world, it is always a good idea to haunt your local bargain bookshop where books that were orginally £25 can often be bought for a much lower sum.

Your own home is also a wonderful source of material for lace-making. Look closely at the food you prepare and eat everyday, even the bubbles in your bath with their rainbow coloured surfaces. Notice the grain of wood on floors and furniture and even the pattern of tiles on the roof. The possibilities for close observation are endless, you only have to look.

into the opening taking care to match the colours of your threads to the work to be framed. The techniques of rag rolling and stippling your mount card or frame are old but very effective ones.

The question of textiles behind glass is a difficult one to answer. I personally don't like the idea of anything covering the textile, however, sometimes a delicate piece of work needs protection from pollution in the atmosphere and some form of clear material must be used. Perspex box frames are ideal for a lot of work but hard to come by.

FIVE

Simple Design Ideas

Having made a promise to yourself to observe your surroundings more closely, you now have the task of making what you see into a workable design for your lace-making.

There can be no greater satisfaction than completing a piece of lace that was your idea and design from its very conception. To be able to design your own piece of lace you do not have to be a graduate from an art college although I would concede that that would help matters greatly! There are many ways in which you can draw out a simple design and then carry out that design as a piece of lace.

We have already discussed the possibility of using a picture out of a magazine, now we will go on to designing some lace from the starting point of a blank sheet of paper. Good stationers and art shops usually stock large selections of drawing and colouring materials. A tin of water soluble pencils and a pack of felt-tip pens in a range of colours would be a good buy. If you are looking for paints then try the Designer's Gouache for brilliant clear colour. These paints are quite expensive so start with the three primary colours, red, blue and yellow. From these colours all other colours are mixed (*see* Chapter 4). Choose a medium sable paintbrush, size 6 series 16 Winsor and Newton is a comfortable size to use. Sable brushes are expensive but very worth while for their fine painting line.

You will also need a range of lead pencils, one each of grades HB, 2B and 3B and a good pencil eraser. A sketch-pad size A4 and a ruler and pair of compasses will enable you to experiment with the exercises discussed here.

Having bought your materials you now need to find out about them. Take the water-soluble pencils, a paintbrush, sketch-pad and some water and just try out the colours on a blank sheet of paper blending them with water to create a softer effect. Take your lead pencils and starting with the 3B, a very soft one, begin by shading in an area on the page, starting with a very firm dark shade and gradually taking the weight off the pencil until it is just stroking the paper. Do this with all your pencils simply to find out what marks they make on the page.

Try out the felt-tips, making marks and shapes on a page. Even if you only scribble be aware of the shapes that you are creating, possibly your next piece of lace.

Try this exercise. Take a piece of fruit or vegetable, an apple, tomato or red pepper. Cut it open down the middle. You are going to attempt to draw the surface that you see. Treat the drawing as a diagram if it makes you feel happier. Observe the surface closely, for all its colours, list the colours and then make a colour winding. Having done this first try to draw the outline and then fill in the centre of the fruit/vegetable in a diagramatic way. Do not worry about shading.

Another simple exercise is simply to let your pencil wander across the page and then draw in a parallel line to the one you have just drawn. Your wavy scribble immediately takes on the form of a flowing ribbon.

Having made your ribbon you could now colour in the spaces made with a pair of complementary colours, for example red and green. The areas of colour could be a corded stitch and the outlining completed in close buttonhole stitch. This design is very reminiscent to those lace-makers among you of the old tape laces where a bobbin lace tape, later machine-made tape, was twisted and turned around a pattern and then joined together with needlelace.

When starting to draw from nature choose an object that has a clear outline and is not too 'busy'. Shown here (Fig 48) is a drawing of a twig with leaves on it. A small 'window' was placed over the drawing to enable a pleasing area to be chosen which would make a design for lace. The design chosen was then repeated in mirror image to give a pattern repeat. Felt-tip pens were used in the outlining and shading of the drawing.

Rough bark can provide a wealth of design material. Not only can you draw directly from the bark but you may also take pencil rubbings from its surface.

Val Palmer has created the effect of bark using

Fig 47. Design taken from twig drawing

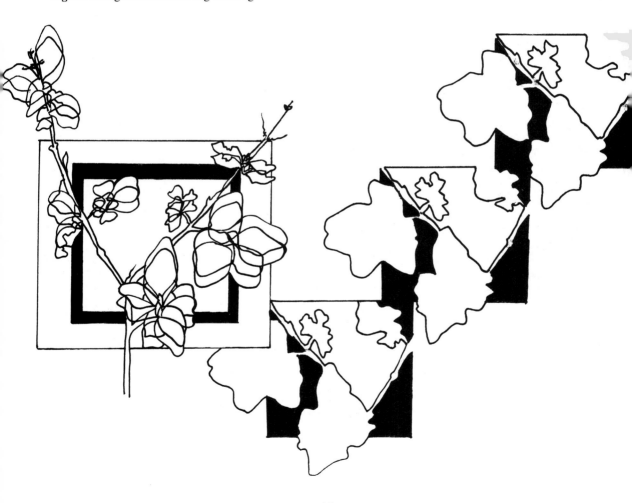

Fig 48. Landscape. Worked by Maureen O'Dwyer in silks. 10cm × 14cm

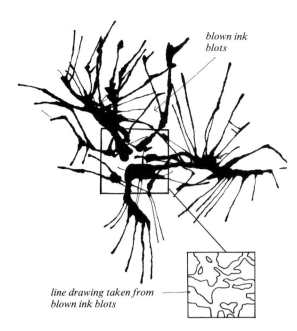

blown ink blots

line drawing taken from blown ink blots

Fig 49. Blown ink blots and line drawing

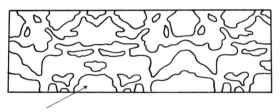

line drawing repeated to make border pattern

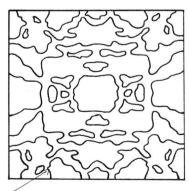

line drawing reversed and repeated to make block pattern

Fig 50. Designs from line drawings in Fig 49

wool and string and then has decorated the 'tree stump' with needlelace leaves (see Figs 1 and 2 in the Introduction).

Design by accident

A very exciting and unpredictable way of obtaining a design is to do so quite by accident. To carry out this exercise you will need three bottles of coloured ink, several blank sheets of paper and three drinking straws. People with high blood pressure should beware, a lot of blowing is required!

Cover your clothes, hands and any nearby furniture, and also cover the surface on which you intend to work with newspaper. Place a sheet of blank paper, at least A4 size, down onto your newspaper-covered table. Open your three coloured inks and taking a straw, immerse one end of it into the ink bottle, place your thumb over the other end of the straw, lift the straw out of the bottle and hold it over the blank paper. Remove your thumb from the end of the straw and the ink being held in the straw will blot onto the paper. Repeat the procedure using the other ink colours. Try to use separate straws for each colour to keep the inks from mixing in the bottles.

Having achieved several ink blots on the paper take a clean straw and blow through it at the ink blots on the paper. You will find that you have to blow quite hard through the straw to make the ink blots move and merge with one another. The colours and line shapes achieved are quite amazing.

You will no doubt want to do this exercise several times to create different effects and colour changes. If you have children ask them to help, they will enjoy it.

When you have accumulated several sheets of 'designs' take your paper 'window' and place it over a favourite sheet, moving it around until you find an area of line and colour that you like. Using a sharp B pencil trace the lines that you see within the square and then around the edge of the square. Turn your tracing over and go over the

48

6
Triangles II. Worked in
silks by the author.
10cm × 6cm

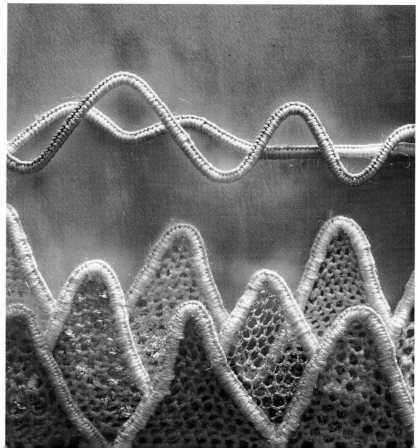

7
Triangles III. Worked in
silks by the author.
10cm × 6cm

8
Space-dyed threads and fabrics

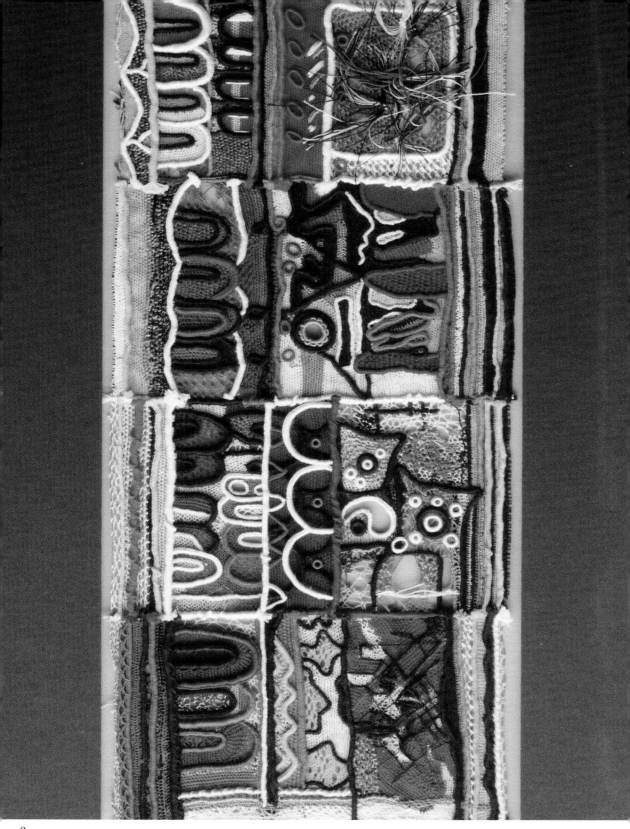

9
Project. Worked in silks by the author, from a design by David Wasley. 20cm × 6cm

10
A close-up of the project shown in colour photo 9.

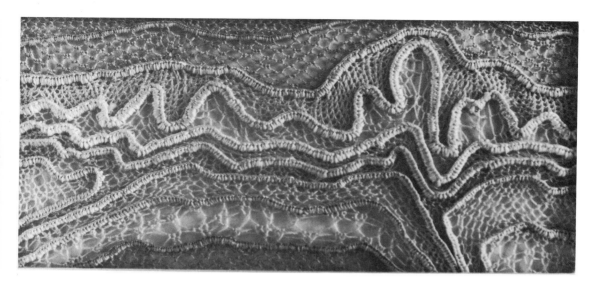

Fig 51. Wave. Worked by the author in silk. 5cm × 9cm

Fig 52. Japanese wave. Worked by Angela Weddell in silk and cotton. 10cm × 8cm

49

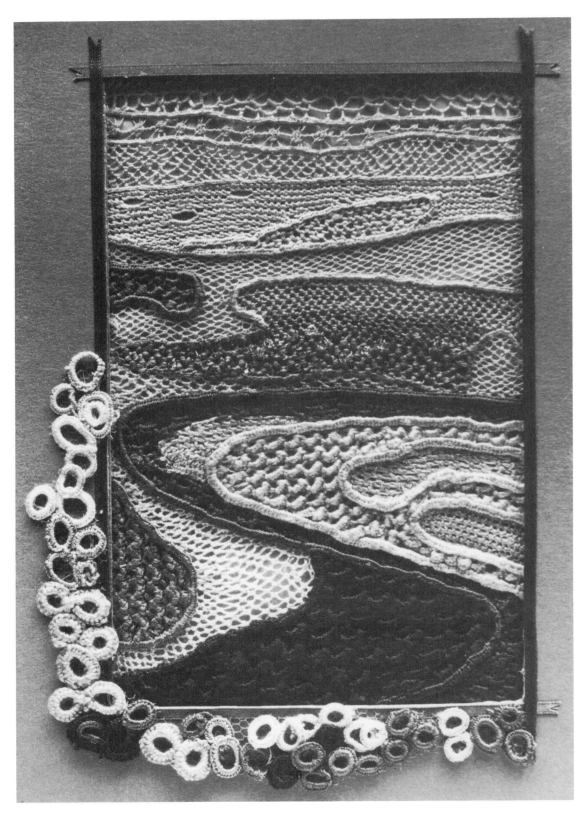

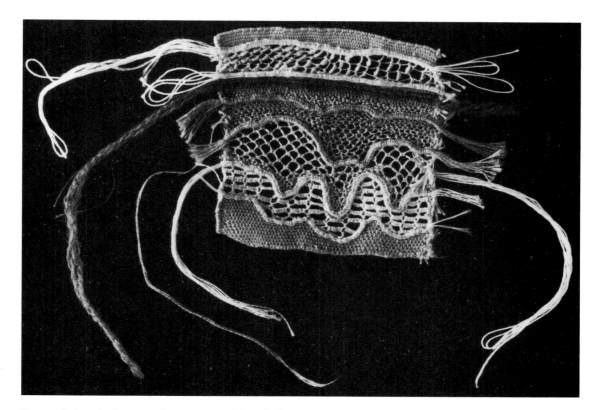

Fig 54. Wavescape. Worked by Mavis Elliott in silk. 5cm × 4cm

lines of the design on the reverse side of the tracing paper. Turn the paper back and then drawing over your original lines transfer the design onto a clean piece of cartridge paper.

To make a mirror image of the pattern, turn your tracing paper over to the reverse side, lay the design next to the one already transferred and draw over the lines of the design again to put a mirrored pattern next to the original.

To make a block pattern trace off the design into four spaces reversing the tracing as you go around the square.

The panel 'Evening Light' is an example of a design taken from a simple leaf and twig shape (*see Frontispiece*). Having made the drawing and tracing the tracing was overlaid on the drawing until a pleasing shape was found. I liked the curves of the leaf shapes contrastng with the upright stems or 'trunks' as they became. To give

Fig 53. Seashore. Worked by Daphne Catling in silk. 16cm × 8cm

more interest to the piece diagonal lines of stitching and shaded silks were used for the background, carried out in single Brussels stitch. Even at this early state in my affair with lace I was very interested in creating textural effects so the 'trees' became decorated with small bundles of yarn knotted onto a ground of single Brussels stitch carried out using a thick wool. The bundles of yarn are several strands of different coloured silk for a shaded effect.

The flower of the Fritillary was the inspiration for the piece of work shown in Fig 6. The Fritillary group is a sub-group of the North Downs Lacemakers. The group encourages its members to design and make their own lace without following someone else's pattern. The first project that was set to make a piece of lace showing the Fritillary in some form. My version became a very close up view of the petals of the flowers. I used double Brussels stitch together with some random stitches to create the effect that I wanted. I managed to find a postcard with a picture of a fritillary on it from which I made some initial sketches and colour windings. The final piece of work was mounted onto a piece of space-dyed silk that seemed to have the colouring that I wanted for the background of the piece.

Nature was also the inspiration behind a series of wave pieces. I had a particularly lovely holiday in Cornwall one summer. A favourite place is the north coast where the Atlantic Ocean crashed onto the slate cliffs of the land. The rolling breakers are a constant source of delight, they are ever changing in colour and shape and are wonderful to ride on. The feeling of bubbling waves around your body is quite addictive! The subtle colours of the sea are all around you from white to deep green. These thoughts were in my mind when I drew up the design for the lace. I wanted to capture the bubbles and the curving lines and the colours.

The Japanese have a particular style of draw-ing waves which lends itself to lace-making. Angela Weddell chose this style for her piece of lace. She has used strong colours and a three-dimensional approach to the work. The foam on the lower left-hand corner of the design is made by putting buttonholed bars, at random, over the surface of the design to great effect. The top section of the wave was made separately and added to the main part of the lace when the cordonnette was applied.

Daphne Catling also chose the shoreline as inspiration. Her work shows the sand after the tide has gone out leaving a trail of pools and seaweed. She has used threads of different thicknesses to accentuate the perspective in the view.

Should you wish to design a piece for a particular room in your house, start by looking at the wallpaper, floor covering, and curtains. Using your paper window pick out a small area of pattern on the fabric/paper and trace it. Make a colour winding to match up the colours of the paper or fabric to the threads that you have and then make your lace in these colours.

Fig 55. Double line sampler design

SIX

Preparing Designs for Lace

I was asked by artist, David Wasley, who currently designs and makes stained-glass windows, to interpret a design that he had painted into needlepoint lace. The design was originally intended to be used as the basis for a stained-glass window but the commission was not forthcoming. David Wasley then decided that he would like to see the design interpreted in several different media, a needlelace and a canvas work version having been carried out so far. See Colour plate 9 and Figs 68b and 88.

Design ideas

If, however, you do not have someone to provide you with designs to work as lace you will need a starting point. Some ideas have already been discussed in previous chapters, here are some others.

Think about what you like best as far as shape is concerned. Do you like circles or squares, sharp triangular points or soft flowing curves, geometric designs or realistic cottage garden shapes? At this point try and be a little adventurous and perhaps plan a piece of work that encompasses shapes that you would not normally choose. It is in this way that you find out about the development of design and how by not being satisfied with what you first thought of you can push your idea further and make it better and more interesting.

Having made the exciting decision to try something entirely new you can now go on to think about what colours you like to use. Be sure

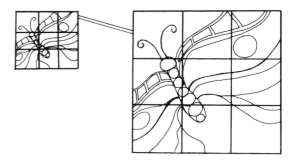

Fig 56. Enlargement of a design

to think really carefully about this. Are you in a colour rut? Do you always pick out the same group of pinks or creams or greens? Now is the time to try for a different selection of coloured threads.

You may now have established that you like soft flowing lines and you like bright colours. If all your magazine cuttings fail you, then you may find a design to your liking in one of the Dover publications. These books are full of design ideas, some of them very suitable for needlelace work. Stained-glass designs are also perfect for lace. They have all the sections of the shape outlined in a heavy black line. These lines would be the lead lines in a stained-glass window, in lace the lines become the cordonnet.

Transferring designs

Having chosen your design you must then transfer it to a piece of paper. It is quite useful to use

53

Fig 57. Punto in Aria. Worked by the author in silks. 4cm high

graph paper on which to draw out your design. The lines on the graph paper give a good guide if it is necessary for the design to be symmetrical. If you have chosen a photograph or part of a picture as your design, you may now trace off the design's shape onto some tracing paper. You do not have to draw the design yourself! You may only wish to take part of a photograph or magazine picture. Take the 'window' you made in the previous chapter and hold this 'window' over your chosen picture. You can move the window around on the picture until you find an area that you think could reproduce effectively as needlelace. Having chosen an area trace the outline of the design onto tracing paper.

Transfer your tracing to a piece of white paper as explained in Chapter 6.

You may want to enlarge the design that you have chosen. This is quite a simple task. Simply draw a grid over the design and then draw another grid to the size you want your finished design to be. Working square by square, copy the original small design into the larger grid. When the design is complete, outline it with a fine, dark

Fig 58. Garden view

felt-tip pen and then rub out the pencil lines of the grid.

When choosing a design to make your first piece of lace try not to have too many lines in it or in fact, too many very sharp angles as these are fairly difficult for a beginner to work. A reasonably flowing shape may be a wiser choice ensuring a long and happy relationship with your needle and thread.

Landscapes are always appealing. They can be drawn out quite simply or traced from postcards or favourite photographs. Pick out the most prominent features to trace, as in this garden view through curving arches of trained apple trees. The border on either side of the path may be given a good deal of interest with the use of coloured and textured stitches.

Geometric shapes are also very pleasing. They can be made up to appliqué onto clothing or as mobiles to hang in a window or over a child's cot. They can be made up like patchwork pieces and put together to form a small wall hanging or even as decoration for cushions or the tie packs on curtains.

You will by now be eager, I am sure, to begin stitching.

Making lace

Stage one
As has already been said you will need to draw out your design onto good quality white cartridge paper. You should make the outline of the design very clear using a fine dark felt-tip pen. Having done this, cut a piece of clear PVC or architects' linen to fit over your design and to overlap the actual drawing by at least 2.5cm. Tack these two pieces of paper down onto three thicknesses of any scrap material, a plain dark-coloured fabric is better than a brightly-patterned one. The tacking stitch should run around the margin that is between your design and the edge of the paper. Stage one is now complete.

Stage two
The whole drawing must now be outlined with a double thread couched down around it, the cordonnet.

Taking a length of thread, it could be any thickness depending on the scale of the piece of work that you have in mind (preferably in a similar colour to those colours being used to make the lace), and fold it in half. Thread a fine sewing needle (as my work tends to be quite fine I use a crewel needle, size 16, with a fine bobbin lace thread in the same general colour as the work), and bringing the needle up through the backing fabric and PVC or linen, pass it through the loop formed by the folding of the cordonnet thread. Continue to couch down the double

Fig 59. Camisole needlelace panel. Worked by the author in silk fabric and threads

cordonnet thread, leaving a space of approximately $\frac{1}{8}$in between each stitch for a firm, continuous outline to the work. If the stitches were any wider apart the cordonnet would develop into a wavy line as the lace is made and the tension of the buttonholed fillings increased.

Intersections

Where you reach an intersection in a design take one of the cordonnet threads (the one nearest to the intersection in the diagram is the right-hand thread), and couch it around the line of the design to point B and then back again to point A. The two original threads now continue to point B where they must be passed through the loop that was formed by the branching thread. This can easily be achieved by threading the cordonnet

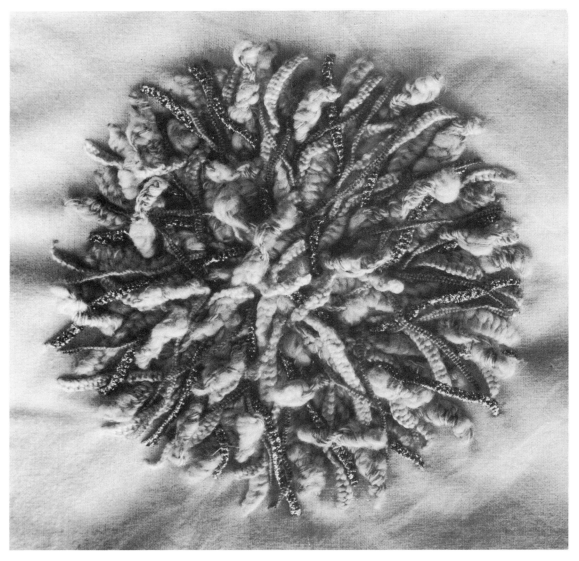

Fig 60. Buttonhole bars. Worked by Jane Sweetsur. 11 × 11cm

threads into a tapestry needle and then passing the needle through the loop, or by using a very fine crochet hook to ease the threads through. This forms a secure join in the cordonnet.

The double cordonnet threads should be kept parallel and flat and not be allowed to twist over one another, they should also be held under an even tension as you work.

Adding in new cordonnet thread

If the cordonnet thread runs out before you have completely surrounded the design, divide the two threads and, laying a new thread, Cl next to one of the old ones (A), couch the two together until the old thread runs out. Lay in a second new thread and continue around the design. A secure join in the cordonnet is essential so that there will be no weaknesses in the outlining of the work. You can now cut off the tail of thread B.

On completion of the piece of lace you will cut

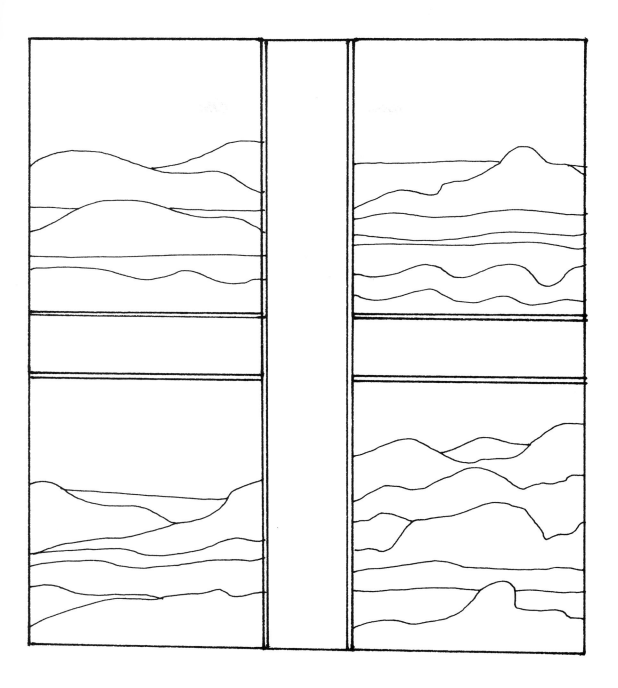

Fig 61. Landscapes to work

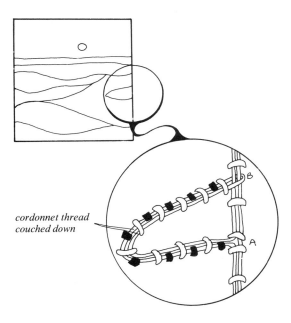

cordonnet thread
couched down

Fig 62. Cordonnet dividing to take in shape on design being worked

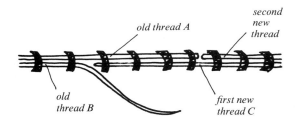

old thread A

second new thread

old thread B

first new thread C

Fig 63. Joining new thread

through these couching stitches that run between the backing fabric and the design.

When the design has been completely surrounded by the cordonnet, the whole thing should then be pinned securely to your pillow. A 1½in-diameter piece of doweling should be pushed underneath the work as an edge to work against. This stick may be moved up and down under-

neath the work as you progress with it.

Stage three—filling in

Having created a solid outline for your design you are now ready to begin filling in the spaces you have created—real painting by numbers! Careful consideration must now be given to colour, size of threads and size of stitches. Hopefully you will already have a colour winding of the threads you want to use to correspond with the design you have chosen. Stick your colour winding onto a sheet of paper and write beside it the names or numbers of the threads, this will enable you to reorder easily if you run out. Having chosen your colours, make further notes on the same sheet concerning the location of each colour and thread in your design.

This preliminary work is very worthwhile; it saves so much time while you are actually working the lace.

The question of where each stitch is to go is a very important one. The whole impact of the work may be changed by using unsuitable stitches. The secret of the matter is density and by that I mean that if you have a very closely stitched area it will appear smaller than an area filled with a very open stitch. You should practise these effects on a sampler. For example draw two oval shapes, and having prepared the cordonnet, fill one oval with dense corded stitches, and the other with an airy open single Brussels stitch. Now look at both. The dense stitching should make the first oval appear to be smaller than the second, although they are, in fact, the same size.

It is important to attempt to create a balance between areas of dense flat stitchery and more interesting areas of complicated stitches.

Simplicity of stitches

Sometimes it is essential to use only one or two stitches when working a design, especially if the design is multi-coloured. The shapes and drama of the design will then shine through and not be lost in many different complicated stitch patterns. The early laces used only corded stitches with a few variations, and achieved miraculous

58

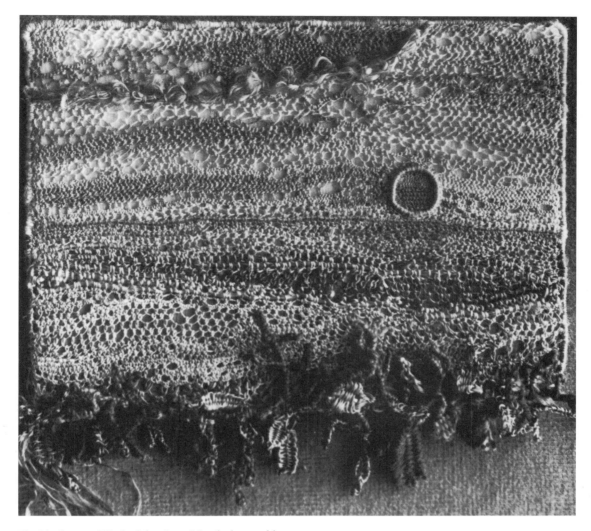

Fig 64. Sunset. Worked by Jane Meade in machine embroidery thread. 7cm × 5cm

results. To begin stitching a filling, thread your needle either with a ballpoint sewing needle or a tapestry needle, depending on the scale of the working thread. Next, pin the work securely to your lace pillow so that both your hands are free to stitch. None of the stitches from now on will pass through the backing fabric, all the work will be done on top of the linen. Use the cordonnet that you have couched down as a framework within which to build areas of stitchery.

Another good reason for working on a pillow is that it enables you to achieve a better tension in your work. When making any textile tension should be even and consistent for a good result. However, you may one day make a piece of work that uses uneven tension to create a certain effect.

In my opinion it is impossible to lay down absolute rules and laws about creating because this immediately stops people creating!

Having threaded your needle make a knot

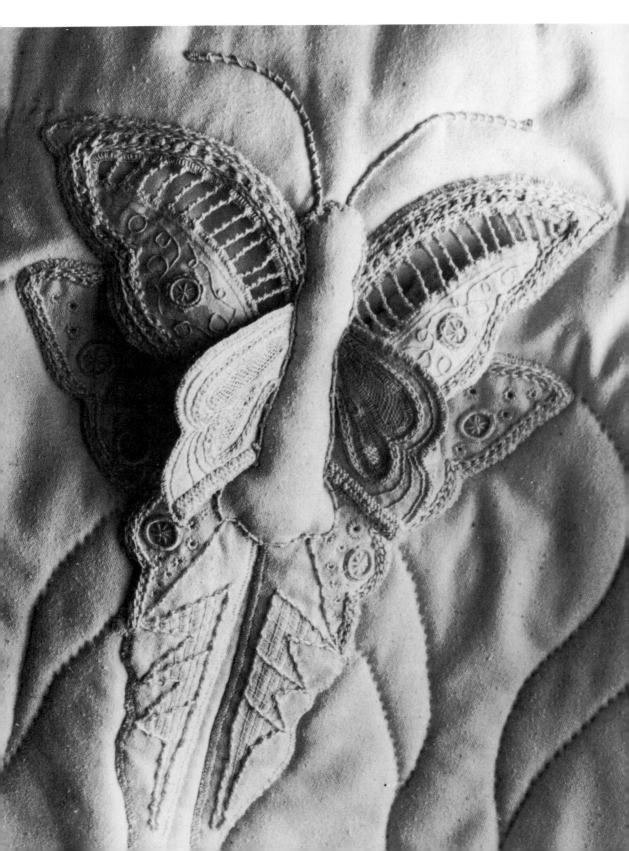

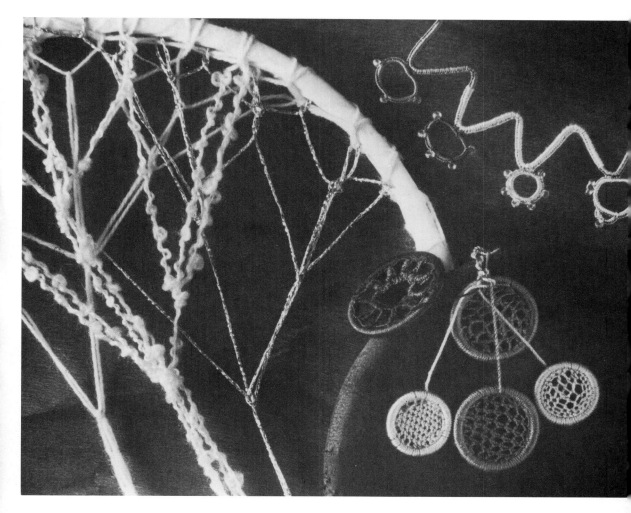

stitch at the side of an area where you plan to start working.

Starting a row of stitches

First rows of stitches

Make your first row of stitches across an edge of the space chosen. They may be evenly spaced or not, depending on the effect you want. As beginners I suggest that you make every effort to space the stitches evenly so gaining control of the technique before you start to stitch at random.

Fig 65. Butterfly Jacket. Worked by Val Fraser in silk and cotton

Fig 66. Circles. Worked by the author, Val Palmer and Rosalie Sinclair

As you make each stitch give your working thread a gentle pull and then hold it down on the work with the thumb or fingers of your free hand. When you make the next stitch repeat this movement. You will gradually get into the rhythmn of working as you continue across the row, and also find a way of holding the needle and thread and of using your fingers in a way that suits you. You will find out for yourself how you like to work and what positions of thread holding will result in the type of work that pleases you.

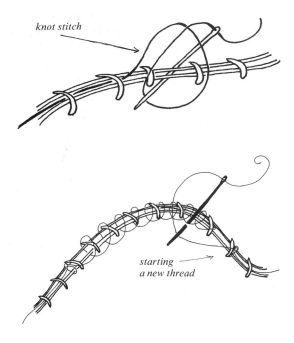

knot stitch

starting
a new thread

Fig 67. Knot stitch and starting a row of stitches

On reaching the end of your row go under and over the cordonnet twice and return across the row you have just made, making your stitches into the loops you have just created.

Ensure that as you start each row you have enough thread in your needle to finish that row. The thread will need to be approximately twice the length of the row to be worked so, if in doubt measure it. Do not join in a new thread in the middle of a row of stitches unless you particularly want a knotty effect; as in the kind of knitting where lots of coloured yarns are used and then joined by a knot, which is then left to the front of the work. This type of work is discussed more fully in the chapter on free stitchery.

To lay in a new thread simply finish off the old one around the cordonnet and put in a new one as you did at the start of the work, then continue to work on all the areas of the design that need filling.

It will soon become apparent that you need to

increase and decrease the number of stitches in a row when working the curved areas of your design.

If you are working a pattern in your stitches and wish to repeat it exactly, it is as well to take some graph paper and note on an outline of the design exactly where new stitches will come in and how the pattern will work into them.

Traditionally needlelace stitches were evenly spaced and the patterns correct in every detail. Whilst having much admiration for this type of work and also feeling that it is essential to practise the techniques in order to try to achieve excellence, I also feel that the lace-maker of today must be allowed to show his/her own creativity in the way in which his/her work is carried out. In other words try not to get bogged down in the technicalities of perfectly evenly-spaced rows of stitchery because you feel that you must copy exactly the techniques of the past to achieve anything. Some may enjoy doing just that but those of you who wish to 'do your own thing' go ahead, for this is the only way that any art or craft form will progress. It may be frowned upon by traditionalists but it will be a contribution to the future. You will find anyway that evenness of stitch and tension will come in time to such an extent that you will long for the days of a freer more relaxed style.

Cordonnette
After filling in all the areas created by the cordonnet it is necessary for the original cordonnet threads, that will by now be almost completely covered in stitchery, to be covered by what is known as the cordonnette.

A pleasing effect will be obtained by using a finer thread in the same or even a contrasting colour to the one that was used for the fillings. You will also need some core threads over which to make close buttonhole stitches.

Traditionally the cordonnette was laid down around the design in the same way as the cordonnet; this was so that there were no weak points to come apart during laundering. However, if you are making a panel or hanging that is not going to be touched let alone laundered, there ceases to be a need for the cordonnette to be applied traditionally. More about this later.

The following method of laying down the cordonnette has been applied to a simple stylized flower shape but can, with a little thought be adapted to your own work.

1. Taking four core threads, crochet cotton is useful here, in a toning colour to that of the work.

2. The threads should be long enough to go around the whole design.

3. Couch two threads around the central ring in the flower.

4. Couch the threads up the side of a petal starting at point A.

5. At point B lay in another pair of threads making four in total.

6. Taking your working thread make eight close buttonhole stitches.

7. Pull gently on the two newly laid threads until they just disappear under the buttonhole stitches just made. Continue stitching around the

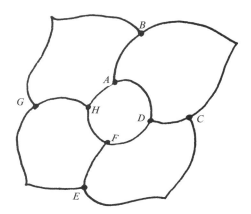

Fig 68a. Flower shape for cordonnette

Fig 68b. Project showing cordonnette. Worked by the author in silk. 25cm × 12cm

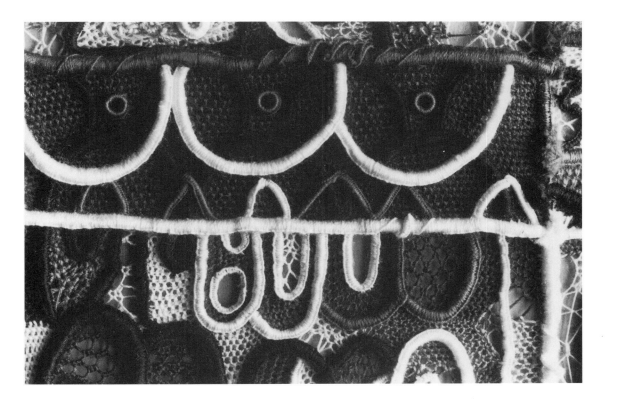

petal or shape.

8. At point C divide the threads. Take two threads and your working thread to point D.

9. Keeping your working thread apart, fold the two core threads back on themselves.

10. Make a knot stitch into the loop just formed.

11. Buttonhole stitch back to point C.

12. Take your needle through the last stitch already at point C. Continue around the next petal using all four core threads.

13. Repeat at points 8–12, at E and at point G.

14. On reaching point B cut off two core threads, take the remaining pair on down the petal to point A.

15. Couch them down around the central ring of the flower on top of the two threads already in place.

16. With your working thread go into the last buttonhole stitch at point B the very first stitch that you worked and then buttonhole to point A.

17. Buttonhole stitch around the central ring of the flower finishing at point A.

18. Finish off your thread underneath the cordonnette.

As you will realise the more core threads put under the buttonhole stitch the fatter the appearance of the cordonnette. Variations on cordonnettes appear later.

Lifting the work

Having completed the cordonnette now comes the most exciting part about your project; the lifting of the work from its background fabric. To do this you need a sharp pair of embroidery scissors with fine-pointed blades if your work is fine. Also a pair of eyebrow tweezers. Take the work and pull apart the linen and paper from the backing fabric. You will clearly see your original couching stitches passing through all these layers. Using your scissors cut through these stitches until the lace separates from the linen or PVC.

At this stage many people worry that the lace will fall apart or that it will shrivel up and die! This should not happen if you have followed the methods of construction closely. If the lace has been made under a great deal of tension then it may shrink slightly when taken off the backing fabric. The back of the work will probably be covered in tiny pieces of the original couching thread. Your eyebrow tweezers should remove these odd bits of thread quite easily.

If you couched your cordonnet using a similar colour thread as the proposed piece of work then any stubborn pieces of thread that refuse to come out, even using tweezers, will not show against the stitchery.

Your piece of lace is now almost finished. The only things left to add are possibly any couronnes that you have made for further decoration. These should be attached to the front of the work using small stab stitches through the fabric of the lace.

SEVEN

Free Stitchery & Textural Effects

You may or may not have come across the words free stitchery. This method of working sounds very appealing as it appears that there are no rules and that you can, therefore, stitch where and how you please. This, however, is not the case. It is essential that the lace-making student should learn the basic traditional skills and stitch techniques of needlelace before attempting to interpret them in a more individual way. It seems that the more rules you learn the more ways you will find to break them.

Having learnt the basics it is a natural development of your work that you should want to put some of your own newly formed ideas and feelings into your craft. Many of us have grown up with the impression that we are not creative. This idea stems from an educational system in which children did as they were told and were not invited to question or reason with their teachers. However, we only have to examine our lifestyles to realise that everyone is naturally creative to a certain degree; it is not necessary to be able to paint the *Mona Lisa* to be creative. As women most of us cook, bear children, garden and paint and decorate our homes. We all buy our own, our children's and, sometimes, our husbands' clothes. We take photographs, write letters and nurture houseplants, as well as entertain friends and decorate the Christmas tree. In all the aspects I have mentioned the element of creativity is present to a greater or lesser degree. We think nothing of putting together an attractive Christmas tree and yet, if someone was to ask us to design a decorated Christmas tree for a piece of needlelace, showing the position and colour of

balls, tinsel and lights, we would throw up our hands in horror and say 'Oh, I'm not the creative type and anyway I can't draw'.

Free stitchery samplers

Unless you choose to mix traditional and free lace stitches together on your original sampler which could look quite delightful, you will need to make up some more bases in order to compare and contrast different thicknesses of yarn when they are stitched together.

Samplers need not be constructional works of art. Use a dark plain fabric as a backing and stitch your tape or ribbon onto it to form a rectangular shape narrow at one end and wide at the other, i.e. about 1in at one end widening to 3in at the base and about 4in long. Make two shapes like this so that you have plenty of space to try out your yarns.

You should now look into your thread box and choose ten threads of different thicknesses for the first sampler. You will be surprised at just how many you have.

Lace-makers amongst you will have a ready-made collection of very fine threads.

If you do not possess any fine lace threads then use an ordinary Sylko sewing cotton. Machine embroidery and metallic threads may also be used. Embroidery cottons and crochet cottons come into the next area of thickness. You could then go on to pick out fine wools, chunky wools, bias binding, seam binding, cotton knitting yarns, such as cotton ribbon and many, many more.

65

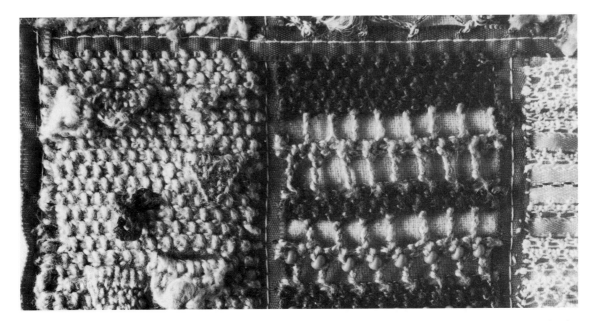

Fig 69. Section of sampler. Worked by Pam Nether in silk and cotton. Whole sampler approximately 21cm²

Fig 70. Section of sampler. Worked by Pam Nether in silk and cotton

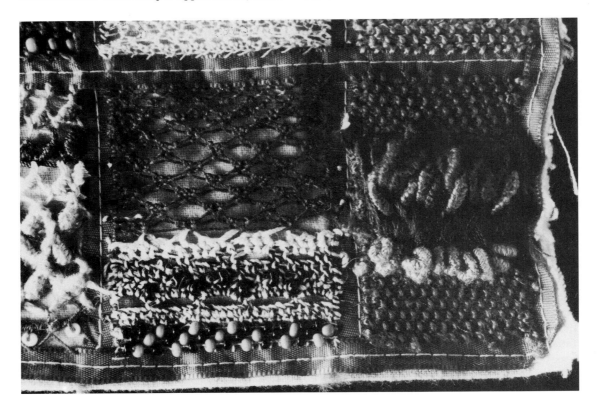

Fig 71. Corded stitch with wool. Worked by the author. 5cm²

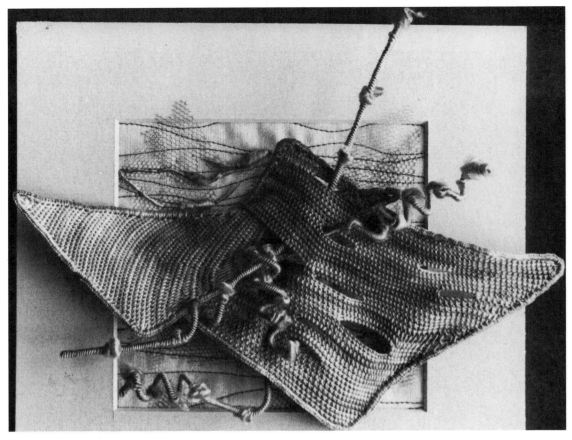

Fig 72. Wired shapes. Worked by Valentina Brunn in space-dyed cotton. 10cm × 10cm

The idea behind all this collecting is that you begin the sampler at its widest end using the thickest thread that you have and after working approximately four rows of single Brussels stitch, change to a slightly finer thread. Work another four rows and change your thread again to something finer still.

The sampler when finished will immediately show you what the different thicknesses of thread look like when stitched into rows. It will tell you whether you like to work with fine threads or thick threads and also whether you like bright colours or pale ones.

You could even cut up strips of fabric and stitch with it as I have done in this sample piece. I very much liked the idea of using the lace stitches as an inset on a jacket sleeve or waistcoat front rather in the way of the slashed sleeves of the eigtheenth century.

Having completed a sampler using the single Brussels stitch you could now go on to experiment with the corded stitch.

Varying the density of your stitchery may be achieved quite simply. Using an empty space on a sampler base make three or four rows of corded stitch across the top of the space. On the fifth row when you return with your buttonhole stitches, miss out every other stitch on the row above. On the sixth row miss out every other stitch on the previous row again. On the seventh row you must now decide either to miss out stitches again or to start to put them back. By altering the number of stitches in rows in this way, you alter the density of the stitching. This could be useful

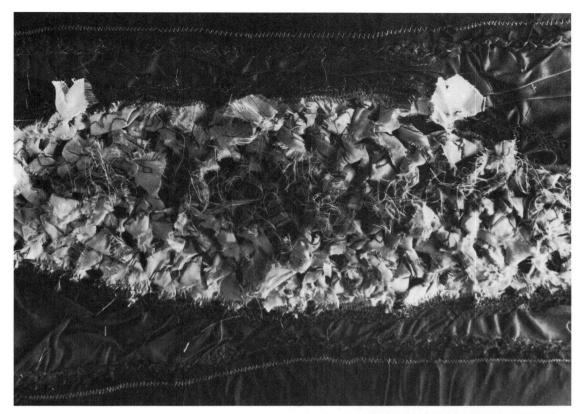

Fig 73a. Silk Insertion. Worked by the author. 19cm × 10cm

Fig 73b. Close-up of Fig 73a

when you are stitching an area of lace that requires such effects, for example in a landscape the horizon line would be very dark and require dense stitches, whereas the middle ground would require a lighter effect.

Another variation on the corded stitch would be to add three or four stitches to a loop occasionally. This gives extra interest and texture to a piece of work and leads you on to create holes in your stitching in random places. These holes can then be decorated further by oversewing with thread, adding beads or couronnes.

Make four rows of corded stitch and then, on the fifth row, miss out three loops and continue. On the sixth row, when reaching the cording not filled with stitches, put in as many buttonhole

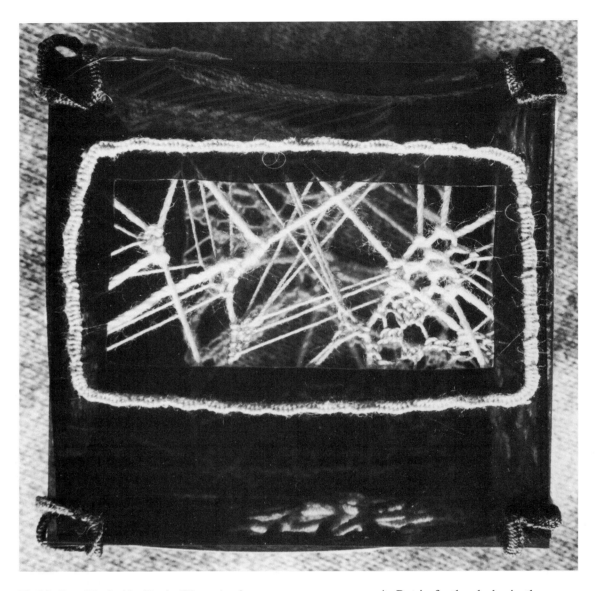

Fig 74. Box. Worked by Denise Watts. 4cm^3

stitches as you can to fill the empty cording. Continue along the row as normal.

Notice that on the row after the creation of the hole not all the stitches on the lower edge of the hole are picked up. You may pick up every other stitch or even every third stitch, depending on the number of stitches required to make a row the same as row A. Put in further holes in the same way.

In the Angel piece I have oversewn holes in the lace with a fine gold thread for decoration, simply running the thread at the back of the work from hole to hole.

Having experimented with the corded stitch you could now try variations on the single Brussels stitch. When sewn traditionally the stitch can be beautiful in its simplicity. To give a contrast, however, try stitching every third or fourth stitch, on the return row perhaps make only one or two stitches into the previous row and take your thread well down the side of your space so that sharp angles are created (see Fig 75b). When used with traditional methods of stitchery this more open work creates an airy effect.

Texture

When stitching a landscape you may find that you would like to create areas of texture in the foreground of the work. You could do this by simply increasing the number of threads in your needle right up to as many as six threads used together and continuing with a normal stitch. However you may wish to actually put stitches

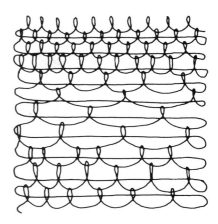

Fig 75a. Dense and open stitchery

Fig 75b. Random stitches. Worked by the author in linen and silk. 5cm × 4cm

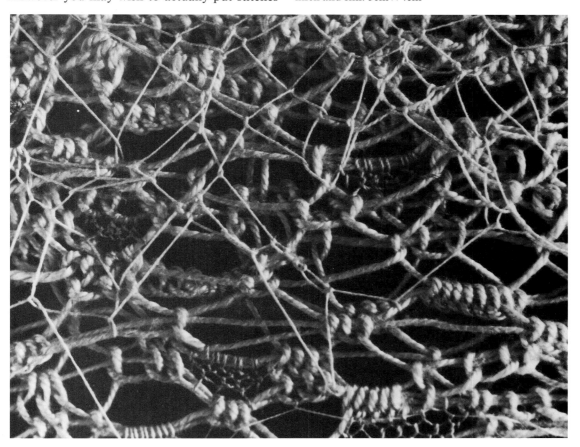

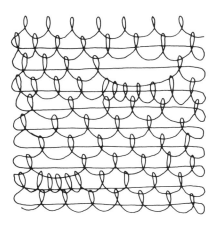

Fig 76. Holes in corded stitch

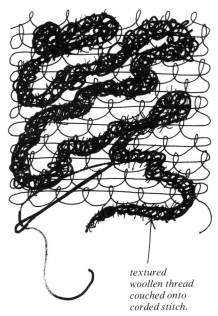

textured woollen thread couched onto corded stitch.

Fig 77. Close-up of Angel piece showing holes in corded stitch. Worked by the author

Fig 78. Couching

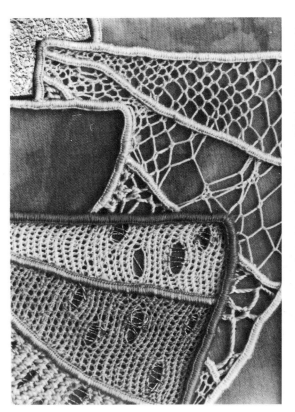

into stitches to give a more 3D effect. There are several ways of doing this.

A simple way would be to couch thick thread that has slubby bits of colour already in it onto an area of plain corded stitching. To couch the thread down begin at one corner of the area that you want to cover. Thread a fine sewing needle with a length of Sylko sewing cotton in the same colour as the thread to be couched. At Point A come up from underneath your corded stitches and catch down the end of the textured thread. Make two more couching stitches along the thread and then turn the thread back on itself to form a curve and to send the thread diagonally across the work (line B). As you continue to couch the thread down you will notice that your Sylko cotton disappears into the yarn and cannot be seen. You should bend and twist your textured yarn so that it completely covers the area you want to fill. An example of a couched thread can be seen in Fig. 8 where a thick hairy thread has been couched onto a single Brussels stitch.

Some points worth remembering concerning couched threads are that you can make dense areas of the thread or simply lines or circles; you

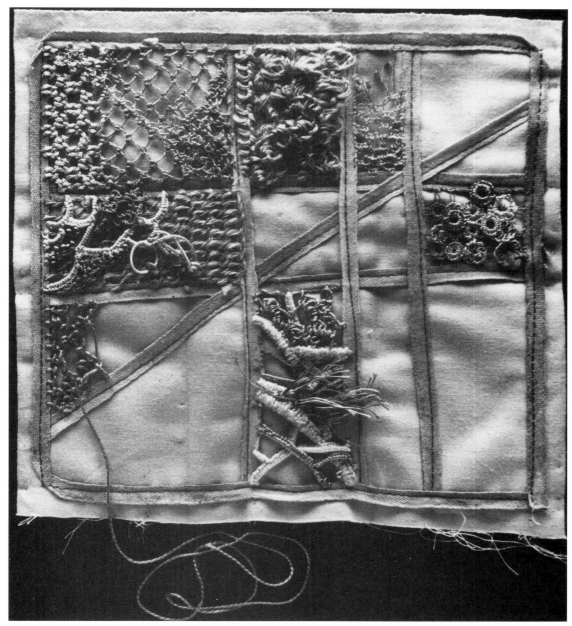

Fig 79. Sampler. Worked by Ann Sutton. 13cm × 13cm

could couch the thread down with a buttonhole stitch; you could force the thread being couched up into a loop between the couching stitches; or you could knot it before laying it down. As well as textured yarn try using other media such as strips of plastic, sequin waste, metal swarf and objects such as shells and interesting pieces of driftwood.

Another way of creating textural effect with a three-dimensional feeling is to make branching bars across the area in several layers, the bars

73

Fig 80. Close-up of Fig 79

ing thread finally down to the cordonnet and buttonhole back to meet the first bar. Continue along the first bar for another dozen stitches and then take off another bar to the cordonnet. This time, when buttonholing this third bar only, come half-way up the bar and take off in another direction with some more laid threads. You will quickly discover that, by turning your work and going in different directions with your laid threads, a very complex ground area will be developed.

To put in the next layer of bars, start in the same way but, as you lay down the threads to be buttonholed, weave them in and out of the bars already stitched.

You may be working on a garden design and want to show a flower border. To give depth and texture to the border it is possible to stitch buttonhole bars at random across an already buttonholed area. When you have prepared this closely-stitched area, choose three shades of a colour that you would find in a flower, for example, the lovely blues of the delphinium. The threads used for the example in Fig 81 were pure silks size 100/3.

Thread up an appropriate size tapestry needle with a needle length of the darkest shade of thread and starting at the left-hand side of the work. Make a knot on the cordonnet, pass the needle under the corded stitching and bring it up to the front of the stitchery a little way from the cordonnet. Make a bar about ⅝in long, or longer, according to the scale of your work, going over and over with your thread at least four times. Pass the needle under the cording again and come up to make another bar. Continue across the work until you reach the cordonnet where you may secure the thread with which you have been working. Using another length of your dark colour, come up at the start of the first bar and buttonhole it. Go down through the corded stitches and come up at the start of the next bar. Buttonhole this bar in the same way. Continue to buttonhole stitch the bars as you make them in the same way.

This is the first layer of bars. Repeat this process using the medium blue colour, overlay-

weaving in and out of each other until they look like a tangled mass of roots. Beads and picots may be added as you work and the layers of bars worked in shades of colour to add to the illusion. The bars are stitched at random starting with a long bar across the space to be filled. The bar, consisting of at least six laid threads in your chosen thread thickness, should be buttonholed for about ten stitches and then another bar taken off in another direction. Pass your needle over and under the cordonnet and then back into the last buttonhole stitch you made. Take the work-

Fig 81. Buttonhole bars on corded stitch. 5cm²

ing the bars one on top of the other. Take care to buttonhole them so that they do not become attached to each other. It is a characteristic of buttonhole bars that they twist around, this actually adds to the textures effect. Finally work some bars in the palest blue colour so that an effect of distance and depth is created. You can then, if you wish, put in some stitchery, random long stitches in two shades of green to cover the base of the bars. To continue the flower border effect, make small couronnes and stab stitch them near and around your stitchery (Fig 81).

Adding small flaps of stitches to a plain area of work is another way of adding texture. Make

your corded stitch in the chosen area in the usual way. Thread your needle with a contrasting colour to the one that you are using and, after securing the thread to the cordonnet, bring your needle up from behind the cording a little way from the cordonnet. Next make six small buttonhole stitches into six loops of the corded area. Turn back and work five stitches into the loops made by the six stitches. Turn again and work four stitches into the previous row's loops. Continue until you have one stitch left. Pass your needle through the back of the little flap created and then through your original cording. Bring the needle up again a few stitches away and repeat the process. Beads could be added to the end of each flap for further interest.

By using techniques found in other crafts you can experiment further with your lace. Far from

Fig 83. Flaps

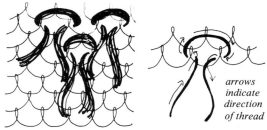

*arrows
indicate
direction
of thread*

Fig 84. Ghiordes knot

Fig 82. Sampler, close-up of Fig 79

corrupting the craft this type of experimental work helps to extend and develop it. Tying on small hanks of yarn to areas of stitchery has already been discussed in a previous chapter. An alternative method of creating a similar effect would be to use a method of knotting that is a weaving technique. The knot is called the Ghiordes knot and is used in weaving to create a pile effect on rugs. To make this knot take a bunch of threads approximately 3in in length. A base of stitchery is necessary to work your knots into, a fairly close single Brussels stitch would be adequate. Pick out a loop in the stitches as shown in this diagram.

Thread a bodkin, or large tapestry needle, with your bunch of threads and, to begin, pass the needle into the middle of the loop leaving a 1in

Fig 85. Landscape—needlelace as detached stitchery on foreground of landscape. Worked by Pam Morgan in silk and cotton. 22cm × 18cm

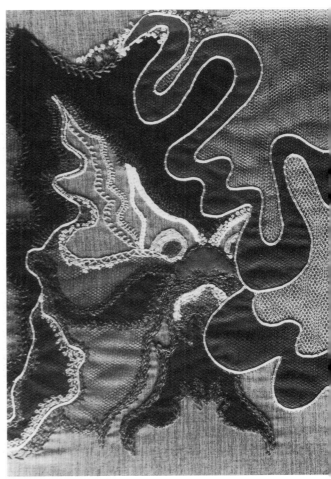

Fig 86. Temper—Nenia told me to write that this is 'the other side of Nenia Lovesey'! Detached stitchery cotton, metallic thread. Approximately 18cm × 15cm

tail, and then under the left-hand side of the stitch. Bring your needle up and over the loop and then enter the loop underneath the right-hand side. Bring the needle up through the middle of the loop and out to the front of the work. Taking the tail that is left and the yarn in the needle, gently pull the knot into place.

This knot would not stand up to heavy wear in this form, and is therefore only suitable for textural effects on lace that is to be used as a decorative accessory.

Detached stitchery may be used in a free and abstract way, as in this piece of work called Temper by Nenia Lovesey.

Gill Martin has used shisha glass and beads to add interest to her piece of work. The design was taken from a cross-section of a plant cell and is carried out to great effect using combinations of buttonhole stitch (Fig 42).

Cordonnette

There are also countless ways in which the cordonnette may be decorated to add interest to your lace. This final outlining of the work is very exciting as it brings your design to life. It covers the cordonnet and with it a multitude of sins!

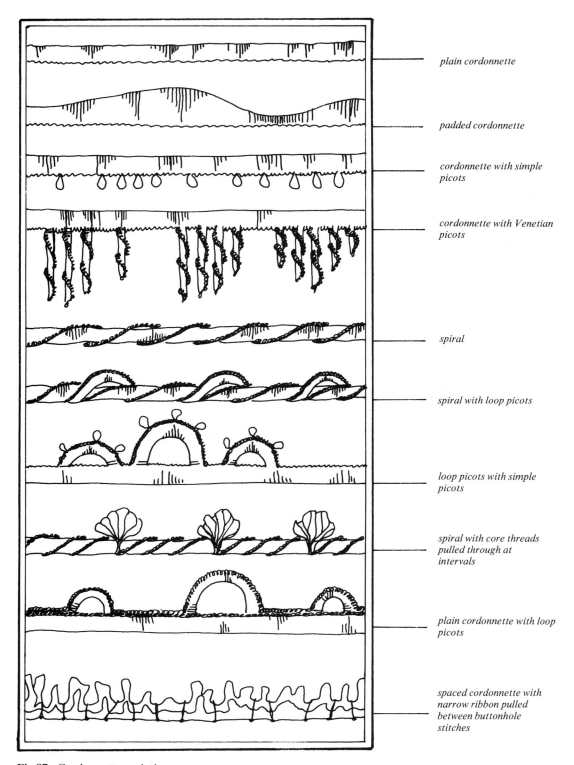

plain cordonnette

padded cordonnette

cordonnette with simple
picots

cordonnette with Venetian
picots

spiral

spiral with loop picots

loop picots with simple
picots

spiral with core threads
pulled through at
intervals

plain cordonnette with loop
picots

spaced cordonnette with
narrow ribbon pulled
between buttonhole
stitches

Fig 87. Cordonnette variations

Fig 88. Project close-up. Worked by the author in silk. 8cm × 6cm. From a design by David Wasley

Different picots can be added; loops, simple or Venetian. You could also add beads, more buttonhole stitches and metallic threads. Core threads can be made to show through the buttonhole stitching in small bunches which may be left as loops or cut to make tufts. If you run a coloured thread through the core it is possible to bring it out at intervals to make picots and then to return it to the core.

Rings can be added to the cordonnette at intervals. These rings can be thick or thin, beaded or plain. They can be made in the same colour as the work or in contrasting colours.

The cordonnette may be given a twisted ap-

pearance with occasional loop picots put in with the twists.

Loop picots of different sizes may be put in at random along the edge of the cordonnette. These loops could also have simple picots on them.

Instead of using threads use ribbon, tape or cord as a core and let it show. Pull this core out in between stitches so that the core thread acts as a decorative feature of the lace (Fig 8, Chapter 1).

These are just a few ideas. I'm sure that as you work your lace projects many more ideas will occur to you, the great thing is to try them and if they appear to work and contribute to the lace then they are quite acceptable.

EIGHT

Tassels & Beads

Another way of creating interesting textural effects on your lace is to attach such things as tassels, beads or even wrapped found objects to the surface of the lace. All these things are simple to make or buy and easy to add to the finished lace piece.

Tassels

Tassels may be bought from upholstery suppliers shops but considerably more interest can be added to your work if you make your own, especially if you use the same thread colours as the piece of work to which they are to be attached.

A simple tassel may be made as follows:

Select a generously-sized bunch of threads making sure that the bunch is nice and chunky. There is nothing worse than a weedy limp tassel! The length of the threads depends on the desired length of the finished tassel, for example for a tassel with a 2in fringe you will need a bunch of threads at least 5in long.

Having cut your threads pick out a finer thread in the same, or contrasting, colour as the main bunch and, using a tapestry needle, begin to buttonhole the central 1in section of the threads.

When an inch of stitching has been completed finish off the working thread by passing your needle back under the buttonhole stitches you have just made.

Taking the buttonhole bunch bend it in half with the knots of the buttonhole stitches to the inside of the bend. Wrap a thread (the same

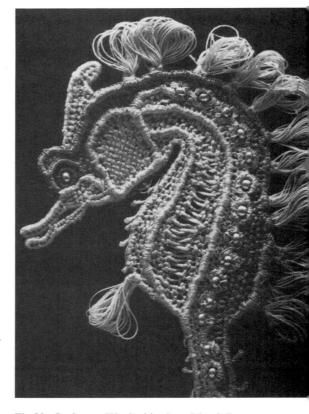

Fig 89. Seahorse. Worked by Jane Mead. 7cm

colour as used for buttonholing) around the threads just underneath the buttonholing. So that no ends of thread show when you have finished this wrapping, make sure you complete the wrapping using the following method:

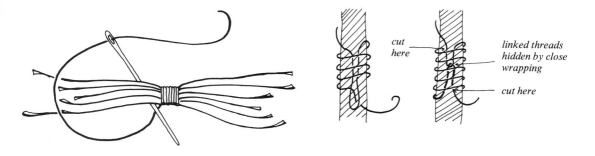

Fig 90. Threads being buttonholed

Fig 91. How to wrap a tassel

Fig 92a. Buttonholed and beaded, wrapped, divided, then buttonholed and beaded, wrapped, divided, buttonholed and beaded, wrapped. **b.** Buttonholed, wrapped. **c.** Buttonholed, wrapped, divided into four, then spiral buttonholing-wrapped. **d.** Folded, wrapped, divided but leaving a central cone, each of four 'legs' wrapped. **e.** Folded, wrapped, some strands knotted and beaded. **f.** Folded, wrapped, central core pushed up, wrapped, core pushed up, wrapped

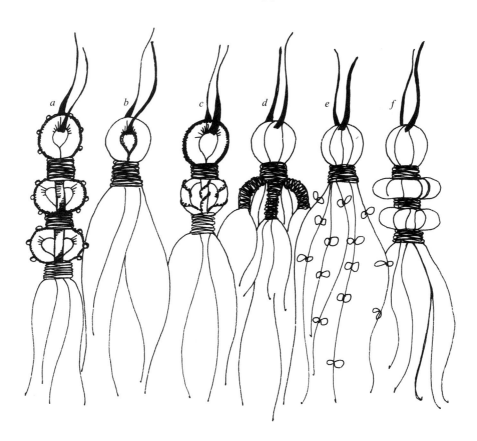

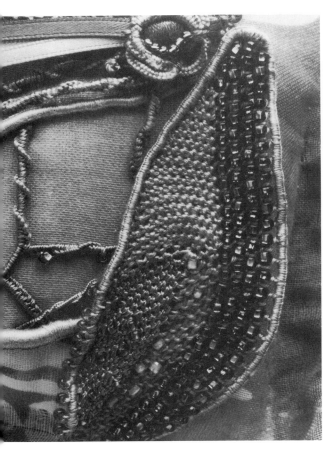

Fig 93. Beading. Worked by Valentina Brunn in silks. 8cm × 7.5cm

You now have a tassel that should look something like the one in the illustration. With practice and a little thought all sorts of combinations of wrapping and dividing of threads will spring to mind. Try to make at least one other tassel from these sketches.

Having made your tassels they can now be added to the lace as decorations on the surface of the lace or as focal points on the corners of work.

Beading

Beading on and in the lace is another way of creating textural effects. Throughout the centuries beads have been used as a means of decoration for clothing and other fashion accessories. They have been applied in patterns to fabric and have been included in knitting, crochet and all other forms of embroidery and lace. The delightful beaded purses of the Victorian era are but one example of the use of beads.

Beaded handbags were common in the 1920s as were beaded dresses, headbands, neckbands and even shoes. An excellent source of study on the subject is the dress collection in the Victoria & Albert Museum where there are many examples of bead-work on view.

When closely sewn with beads a fabric takes on a wonderful drape and 'handle'. The weight of the beads feels luxurious and their glittering quality is both exciting and eye-catching. How, therefore, can beads be used today to increase the decorative quality of needlelace? In fact they are very easy to apply to lace and may be sewn in as you work or stitched in later.

Equipment

You will need to invest in a needle that will pass through the hole in the beads you intend to use. Millward make some lethal looking beading needles in packs of four for very fine beadwork. If your work is on a larger scale then any needle may be suitable.

Sources of beads are also plentiful. Local jumble sales may prove useful, but you must be quick off the mark to secure any bargains.

1. Taking your working thread and making a long loop, lay the loop along the bunched threads with the loop at the skirt end of it and the loose end at the head.

2. Wind the thread tightly around the loop and bunched threads until you have the desired length of winding at the 'neck' of the tassel.

3. Pass the end of the thread that was being wound through the loop that should be sticking out of the base of the tight winding.

4. Pull gently on the free end of thread that remains at the top of the winding, this should pull the loop, as well as the thread, underneath the tight winding. Cut off the pieces of thread still showing close to the wound area.

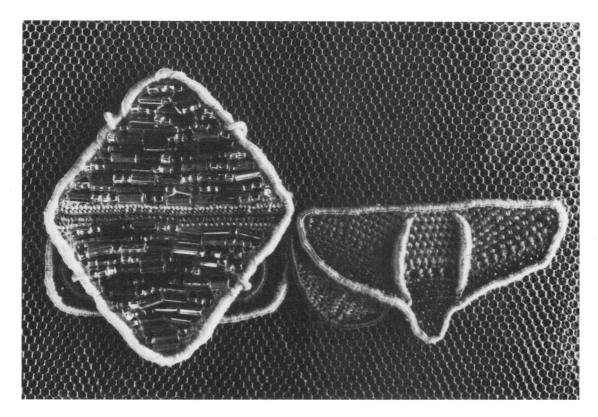

Another source is the bead shop in Neal Street, Covent Garden. Surrounded as you will be by thousands of glittering beads it is difficult to choose which to buy. Unless you have limitless funds, try to decide before you visit a bead supplier exactly what it is that you want. You will not then be sidetracked into spending a fortune. Most local needlecraft suppliers have some sort of bead stock, but for special colours and shapes a visit to a specialist is called for.

Having carefully chosen some beads and threaded a needle, you are ready to begin. If you wish to add beads to a single Brussels stitch area in the lace, make the first row of stitches in the normal way. On the return row make your first buttonhole stitch into the first available loop. Thread a bead onto the needle and then make your next buttonhole stitch into the next loop. It is important to space your stitches far enough apart for the beads to be accommodated easily in the space between the stitches.

Fig 94. Beading on purse flap. Worked by the author. 10cm × 4.5cm

Fig 95. Beads on single Brussels stitch

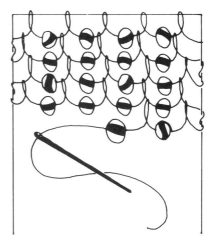

83

On the third row make your buttonhole stitch into the loop to the left of the bead. On the fourth row make your stitches into the loops to the right of the beads in the previous row.

Beaded corded stitch

To bead a corded stitch make your first row of buttonhole stitches as normal, go under and over the cordonnet and then thread enough beads onto the working thread as is needed to fill the row. Return the working thread with the beads to the opposite side of the space being filled and whip down the cordonnet. On the third row make your buttonhole stitch as normal, picking up the loop in the first row and going between the beads to pick up the thread of the second row. Make the next stitch in the same way. The size of the bead will again determine how many will fit between each loop.

A needlelace stitch called Festonsteek found in the Dutch publication *Naaldkant* by Gineke Walvisch-Root is shown beaded. A row of buttonhole stitches are made with a bead in every loop. On the second row the buttonhole stitch is made into each of the stitches in the first row. The third row is made into the knots of the stitches in the second row and is beaded in the same way as the first row.

Bugle beads

To attach bugle beads to the work so that they dangle from the surface pass the needle and thread through the bugle bead, pick up a small

Fig 97. Beads on picots

round bead and then go back through the bugle. The small round bead acts as a stop to the thread being pulled out of the bugle. Make your buttonhole stitch as normal.

The cordonnette and couronnes may also be beaded in a number of different ways. As you buttonhole stitch the cordonnette over laid core threads you could put in a bead on every other knot. Beads may be added to the ends of Venetian and other picots and to the decorative rings around the cordonnette. Couronnes look particularly pretty with beads knotted into them at intervals.

When making tassels or cords, beads may be knotted into them to give extra weight and importance.

During the mid-sixteenth century Venetian

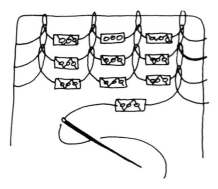

Fig 96. Dutch buttonhole stitch

ladies of the court wore jewelled and embroidered edgings round the low necklines of their gowns. These were called *bavarii*. Needlelace versions of this fashion were designed by two Italian designers, Ostaus and Vercello.

These edgings may or may not have been bead and jewelled. The Venetian necklines of the period did not come above the level of the arm pits so presumably the *bavarii* were worn for the sake of modesty as well as for beauty and decoration. We could quite easily copy that fashion for today's low cut ballgowns and/or party dresses.

All-over beading on garments is very much in fashion in the 1980s so why not try a few beads yourself?

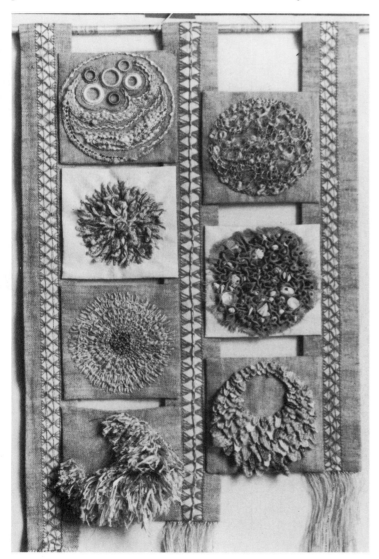

Fig 98. Hanging. Worked by Jane Sweetsur in linen, wool and metallic threads. Each section approximately 12cm²

85

NINE

Dyeing

Fig 99a. Frame. Worked by the author in silk and wool. 10cm × 10cm

I have included the subject of dyeing in this book because I feel that it is an important aspect of any needle craft which not enough people know about.

Most of us have ventured into the world of 'dyeing it yourself' at some time or other. We usually associate the word 'dyeing' with boiling pots of colour teetering on the cooker making the kitchen look and smell like a sorcerer's cavern! However this method is not suitable for dyeing small quantities of fine threads. The main method that will be discussed in this chapter is that of cold water dyeing which is quick, clean and easy to use.

Other methods of dyeing yarns are, therefore, hot water or direct dyeing and dyeing by using natural substances—vegetable dyeing. The best thing about vegetable dyes is that the quality of the colours produced on the yarns are almost impossible to copy using chemical dyes. Some textile artists would not consider using chemical dyes for this reason.

Before dyeing yarn with vegetable dyes it has to be treated with a mordant, that is a chemical that prepares the yarn to receive the dye. Different mordants will produce different colour results using the same dye. Mordants most commonly used are alum, which gives a bright colour to the yarn, chrome giving a duller effect and iron giving darker greens, greys and browns. Mordants may be bought from your chemist or craft shops. They should be kept in a secure dry place away from children. When the yarn has been treated with the mordant it is then ready for dyeing.

Onion skins can give different shades of orange and yellow from a deep orange to a more golden colour to a dark brown depending on the mordant used.

Collect enough onion skins to fill a large pan. You should press them down into water with the yarn to be dyed. Bring the water to the boil (there will be an oniony smell) and simmer until the yarn is strongly coloured. Remove the yarn and rinse it well until the water runs clear.

There are hundreds of dye recipes and virtually any plant or vegetable may be used to dye

Fig 99b. Frame, close-up of leaves

yarn, however, do remember that it is illegal to take plants from the countryside so it is best either to grow your own plants to use for dyeing or to buy your dyes from craft suppliers. A very informative booklet called *The Use of Vegetable Dyes* by Violetta Thurston, published by Dryad Press is well worth buying for further information on the subject.

Hot water dyeing

Hot water or direct chemical dyes can be bought from craft suppliers or hardware shops. You do not need to mordant your yarn before using this method of dyeing, but you do need pans of boiling water into which first the dye and then the yarn is put.

It is possible to create a rainbow effect on your yarn using the hot water methods. Dry dye colours are sprinkled onto yarn in a pan. The contents are then simmered in water without stirring. The yarn is removed and rinsed. An exponent of this method is Shirley Simpson who calls the method Rainbow Dyeing. This method gives wonderful colours to fleece before it is spun.

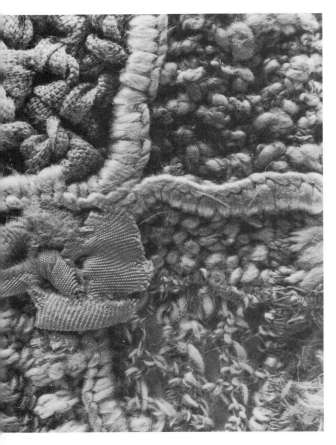

Fig 100. Small sampler. Worked by the author in wool, cotton tape, thick silk, mohair. 5cm².

Cold water dyeing

I think the simplest and most exciting way to dye yarns and fine threads is to use a cold water fibre-reactive dye. You can do away with messy pans and steaming kitchens. You don't have to hunt out specialist shops to find the dye, just your local hardware shop which is bound to stock the Dylon cold water dye range. Examine the tin of dye carefully to ensure that it is actually a cold water dye—the packaging is very similar to hot water dyes. These small tins of dye powder are relatively expensive but you only need the three primary colours to mix together for all the other colours in the colour wheel. Suitable red, blue

and yellow dyes in the Dylon range are Mexican Red, French Navy and Sahara Sun.

Other items needed for a dyeing session are rubber gloves; some plastic teaspoons; a flat shallow dish—glass, plastic or an old meat tin; an apron; and plenty of old newspaper to cover your working surfaces.

Collect together an assortment of fabrics and threads with which to experiment. Those yarns made of cotton, linen, silk and viscose will give good results. Machine-washable wool will also dye well. Jute, hemp and raffia provide scope for colouring textured yarns.

Cultivate the habit of looking into bargain bins in wool shops and haberdashery departments for odd balls of silk mix and viscose yarns, ribbon, and bargain buys of large balls of crochet cotton in pale colours. These will top dye very well. It is often possible to pick up real bargains in this way, normally expensive yarns can be found for as little as 50p each. Jumble sales are another favourite hunting ground.

The yarns should be wound into several small hanks for experimental dyeing and into larger hanks for specific pieces of work that will need a large quantity of thread.

The hanks should be tied safely with spare pieces of thread using the figure of eight method. This helps to keep the threads in the hank tidy and in order while the dyeing is in progress. Take care, however, not to tie the figure of eight too tightly, as when the hank is immersed in the dye stuff the tied area will be unable to absorb the dye easily. The next step is to wash the yarns and fabrics to be dyed in hot soapy water to remove any grease or dressing. If you intend to use calico you will have to soak it well and then run it through the washing machine's hottest wash cycle to ensure that all the dressing in the fabric has been removed. If you did not do this the dye would 'take' in patches on the fabric.

Very fine thread may be dyed but it should first be wrapped around a ruler or a short length of plastic piping before you begin the dyeing process. This may then be dunked in soapy water and rinsed, the fine thread kept in order on its holder. You should now have a pile of damp steaming yarn, not too wet and not too dry.

The dye itself should be prepared in the following way. Firstly you will need to prepare two solutions that assist in the dyeing process. There is no need to buy the fixative that you will be offered when you buy your pots of dye. You can make your own easily and cheaply.

The two solutions required are a salt solution which will drive the dye into the fibres of whatever you are dyeing and a soda solution which is poured onto the fibres to 'set' the dye and prevent it from being washed out.

To make the salt solution, weigh out 4oz cooking salt and mix it with 16 fluid oz of hot water until it dissolves. When it is cool pour it into a large plastic container. Old squash bottles, clearly labelled, are good for this purpose. Make up a separate solution of soda in the same way. As these solutions can be kept indefinitely it is a good idea to double and treble the quantities and make up a large quantity in one go. It will be there when you need it at the next session. Make sure the bottles are clearly labelled and stored in a dry place out of reach of children.

Having made your solutions you can now make up your dyes ready to use. Take approximately half a teaspoon of each of the three colours of dye that you have and mix them separately in three jam jars, using a separate plastic teaspoon for each colour, with a little hot water to dissolve the dye initially. A smaller amount of dye will give a paler colour and more dye a darker colour. Having dissolved the dye half fill the jar with the salt solution that you have prepared. The tin of dye remaining may be sealed up with Sellotape.

Dyeing method

You should now arrange four or five small damp hanks of yarn, one each of cotton, linen, silk mix, viscose and machine-washable wool, in your shallow dish. Choose a colour and begin to spoon teaspoonfuls of dye at random over the yarn, putting the colour in three or four areas. Take another colour and then a third and do the same thing again. You can use your spoon to press the dyes into the yarn and one another but

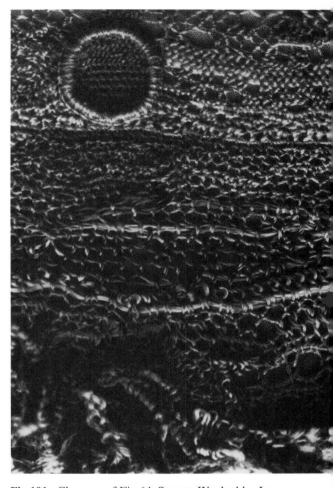

Fig 101. Close-up of Fig 64, Sunset. Worked by Jane Meade

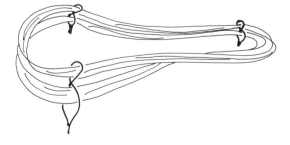

Fig 102. How to tie a hank for dyeing

89

do not do this for too long as all the colours will merge into a dull sludge colour. Now is the time for patience as you must leave your threads for ten minutes to allow the dye to penetrate the fibres of the yarns. This ten minutes seems like ten years when all you want to do is to wash the yarns and see what colours you have!

The soda solution should now be poured over the dye and the dish left again, for 15 minutes this time. Do not worry that the pouring on of the soda solution will further mix the colours, they have already been fixed by the salt in the original ten-minute waiting time.

When the 15 minutes is up pour away the soda and dye and rinse the yarns until the water runs clear. The yarns should then be washed in hot soapy water and rinsed again. You will now have some wonderful random coloured yarns.

Particular yarns that take the dye well are DMC Coton à Broder white; machine-washable, wool; silk mix yarns; the many cotton slub yarns around, for example cotton top; crochet cotton in all thicknesses; and DMC Cordonnet special. Many yarns are a mix of natural and man-made fibres and produce very interesting effects when dyed. For example if cotton is mixed with some other man-made fibre, the cotton will dye whereas the other fibre will not, giving a stripey effect.

Experimenting

Once you have mastered the basic dyeing techni-que you can then start to experiment with the process. For example if you want very distinct areas of colour, the soda solution can be mixed with the dye in the empty jam jar before spooning it over the yarns. This also avoids the need for that ten minute fixing time. All kinds of other variations in the timing, quantities of dye used and colours used will produce different results.

To dye fabrics of silk, cotton, linen or viscose simply follow the above method. Wonderful marbling effects can be achieved and provide an instant source of design inspiration and, of course, background fabric on which to mount your lace. This method of dyeing is almost completely random in that you never quite know just how the yarns will turn out but that, I think, is part of the fun. It is a very worthwhile task to keep a dyeing notebook in which you can note down any special happenings in the dye bath, together with samples of yarn stapled to the page.

To add to the fun, arrange a morning with a few friends who have a similar interest when you can get together with yarns and dyes in someone's kitchen and experiment. It is great fun and you will all benefit from seeing each other's results. It never ceases to amaze me that in a room of 12 students all following the same procedure, no two sets of coloured threads will be the same. Seeing other people's results can inspire you to try, try again!

TEN

Conclusion

Carrying on a Great Traditional Craft

As a medium for expressing individual creativity, needlelace stands tall alongside all other forms of textile creation. The fact that you are creating a textile and not putting threads into another textile, as with embroidery, should not be forgotten. It has been said that in order to remain 'Lace' needlelace should be fine and small but I feel that to put any kind of restriction on the craft is too limiting. In fact I find restrictions of any sort too limiting! I have been called open minded which I regard as a compliment as I feel that you should at least try something before saying that it does or does not work.

The most interesting effects I have achieved have occurred as a result of experimenting with needle and thread at some quiet moment with no thought of an end product, merely an expression in colour, thread thickness, shape, tension and dare I say it, feeling.

To persist and not be content with a first attempt has brought its own pleasure although complete satisfaction with a piece of work seems to elude me! The placing of a needle through a loop again and again has a peculiar appeal, something to do with endorphins I am told, that is, a chemical that is released in your body when you are doing something that is pleasurable. The desire to make lace never seems to diminish, in fact, for me it seems to increase as time goes by.

Needlelace has a glorious past. The meticulous work that was carried out all those centuries ago by clever and hard-working lace-makers will never be repeated. There are very few people today who would sit for 12 hours a day for five, six or seven days a week, year after year in order to produce the yards, swathes and extravagent gowns that were the product of such labour. At least the work was appreciated, treasured and cared for.

Somehow over the centuries the arts and crafts have become divided, those in the art world regarding the craftsman as someone who wears a dirty overall and struggles with rather unpleasant tools and materials to create something that the artist has designed. The craftsman himself is not given any credit for creativity, he is merely considered to be the instrument that brings the artist/designer's work to life. Today we have the opportunity to break away from this label of 'mere craftsperson'. We see recognition being given, if slowly, to embroiderers and weavers.

Lace is enjoying a great revival in this country and abroad. It is therefore vital to take this golden opportunity as lace-makers to train ourselves to be aware of the design factors involved in making lace. Do not be afraid of trying new ways of doing things. There is no need always to copy the old designs and be a mere instrument of the designers of long ago.

We may find that soon needlelace will need to be called by a different name; textile construction, fibre art? The emphasis has moved from the number of stitches we can do to the square inch of lace to how those stitches are arranged. We should not worry about getting exactly the right number of stitches to a row but how that row of stitches looks next to its neighbour with regard to density, colour and texture of the design overall.

We have many amazing materials at our disposal today. We do not have the fine needles and threads of past years but we do have such things as fibre optics, wire, acetate, silks and cottons and wools together with all the exciting man-made fibres and endless other found objects that we might use to create and devise the lace of the future.

Peter Collingwood said in 1960 when he was in the process of devising new methods in his own craft of weaving, 'start with what the technique gives willingly and from those elements construct your design ... the design must so incorporate the technique's peculiarities that one could not be imagined to exist without the other'. The challenge to be both artist and craftsperson is there to be taken up, my hope is that we will all take it up with eagerness.

Appendix—List of Laces

There are many types of needlelace, the following short list gives an indication of the tremendous variety.

Alençon	Needlelace with net rivalling Venetian Point
Aloe Lace	Made from the fibres of Aloes
Argentan	French needlelace fine buttonhole ground
Asbestos	Made from the fibres of asbestos
Brussels	Point de Gaze
Burano	A grounded Venetian Point
Carnival Lace	Venetian Point
Caterpillar Lace	Made of rolled out paste, the pattern on which is oiled so left intact and the ground eaten by caterpillars
Colbert	Point d'Alençon
Coralline	Venetian lace with coral-like pattern
Dentelle	Lace with net ground such as Point de Gaze
Drawnwork	Needlework on linen with drawn threads
Point d'en l'air	Ancient needlelace
Flanders	One of the first needlepoints
Flat Point	Flat Venetian needlepoint
Point de Gaz	Modern Belgian needlelace
Gros Point de Venise	Venetian Point
Guipure	Lace with bar on open ground such as Venetian, Bruges or Maltese
Hair Lace	Human hair
Point d'Irlande	Needlepoint Venetian style
Irish Rose Point	A flat needlepoint
Lacis	A darned net
Manilla Lace	Made of grass in the Phillippines
Renaissance	A needlelace with machine-made braid
Sedan Lace	Needlelace of bold design
Wiltshire	Seventeenth- and eighteenth-century made needle and bobbin lace

Suppliers List

Any good haberdashery department will stock needles, pins, embroidery cottons, sometimes pure silks, textured threads in the form of knitting wools, scissors, calico.

Stationers should stock cartridge paper, drawing pencils, colouring pens and pencils, sticky-backed film of some sort.

The following list of suppliers stock more specialist threads etc. in wider ranges of colours than you may be able to find in the shops.

Mr Brown
Temple Lane Cottage
Little Dean
Gloucestershire GL14 3NX
Tel: Little Dean 22585   Postal Service

Ring sticks and lace pillows

Larkfield Crafts
4 Island Cottages
Mapledurwell
Basingstoke
Hants
Tel: Hackwood 6585   Postal Service

DMC threads, pure silk threads, Gütterman in two thicknesses and a wide range of colours, Metler threads, cotton, needles

Shades
57 Candlemas Lane
Beaconsfield
Bucks HP9 1AE
Tel: Beaconsfield 2956

Small quantities of hard to come by embroidery items available by mail order, including Madeira 'Tanne' 100% cotton in 30, 60 and 80. SAE for details.

The Drawing Board
Wokingham
Berks   Personal callers only

Architects' linen.

General suppliers

A Sells
'Lane Cove'
49 Pedley Lane
Clifton
Shefford
Beds

Equipment, threads and books

Mace and Nairn
89 Crane Street
Salisbury   Wilts

Threads and equipment

Teazle Embroideries
35 Boothferry Road
Hull
North Humberside

Needlepoint lace specialist

Sebalace
76 Main Street
Addingham
Ilkley   West Yorks

All lace-making requisites

Silks & Silk
Jack Piper
Silverdale
Flax Lane
Glemsford
Suffolk

Bibliography

Churchill Bath, Virginia, *Lace*, Penguin Books, 1979

de Dillmont, Thérèse, *Encyclopaedia of Needlework*, DMC

Earnshaw, Pat, *Lace in Fashion*, Batsford

Fisher, Jennifer, *Braid Lace for Today*, Dryad Press

Fisher, Jennifer, *Torchon Lace for Today*, Dryad Press

Groves, Edna, *A New Approach to Embroidered Net*, Dryad Press

Holmes, Doreen, *Flowers in Needlepoint Lace*, Dryad Press

Lovesey, Nenia, *Introduction to Needlepoint Lace*, Batsford

Lovesey, Nenia, *Technique of Needlepoint Lace*, Batsford

Lovesey, Nenia, *Creative Design in Needlepoint Lace*, Batsford

Lovesey, Nenia, *Punto Tagliato Lace*, Dryad Press

Lovesey, Nenia and Barley, Catherine, *Venetian Gros Point Lace*, Dryad Press

Sorenson, Veronica, *Modern Lace Designs*, Batsford

Sutton, Edna, *Bruges Flower Lace*, Dryad Press

Walvisch-Root, Gineke, *Naaldkant Speels en Luchtig* (Needlelace designs and stitches), Cantecleer bv, de Bilt, 1982

Withers, Jean, *Mounting and Using Lace*, Dryad Press

Index